CREATIVE PARTNERSHIPS IN PRACTICE

Developing creative learners

David Parker

B L O O M S B U R Y

LONDON • NEW DELHI • NEW YORK • SYDNEY

Published 2013 by Bloomsbury Education
Bloomsbury Publishing plc
50 Bedford Square, London, WC1B 3DP

www.bloomsbury.com

ISBN 9781441109224

© David Parker 2013

A CIP record for this publication is available from the British Library.

10 9 8 7 6 5 4 3 2 1

Typeset by Fakenham Prepress Solutions, Fakenham, Norfolk, NR21 8NN
Printed by CPI Group (UK) Ltd, Croydon, CR0 4 YY

This book is produced using paper that is made from wood grown in managed, sustainable forests. It is natural, renewable and recyclable. The logging and manufacturing processes conform to the environmental regulations of the country of origin.

To see our full range of titles visit www.bloomsbury.com

Contents

Contents

Acknowledgements

Creative Partnerships was a large-scale undertaking and involved many thousands of people – far too many to list individually. This book, similarly, draws on work that is truly a collective effort and it is difficult to single out individuals and particular groups to acknowledge.

However, it would be remiss not to acknowledge the combined efforts of all the head teachers, teachers, teaching assistants, artists, creative workers, parents and, of course, children and young people that collectively made Creative Partnerships the great success it was. Their efforts helped make thousands of classrooms more creative and guided hundreds of thousands of learners towards more fulfilling experiences in school.

All of the researchers and evaluators who helped inform and develop Creative Partnerships as it evolved over the decade it was running also deserve thanks. Their thoughtfulness and objectivity certainly helped improve the quality of the projects in schools and through an array of research reports, published articles and provocative essays they continue to contribute to the legacy of the programme. Particular thanks are due to those researchers whose projects helped contribute to understanding particular thematic impacts such as well-being, school ethos, learning progression and staff development, many of which form the focus for chapters in this book.

Finally, the Creative Partnerships staff themselves, those in the local offices that stretched from Cornwall to Northumberland and all points in between, all the national office staff, particularly the national director, Paul Collard, who helped shape the programme from 2005 onwards as well as Anna Cutler and Chris May who invested so much time and effort around programme evaluation along with Naranee Ruthra-Rajan and Julian Sefton-Green who helped keep the research programme robust and integral to the development and improvement of the whole programme, thanks are due to this very special group of people whose motivation and commitment to creativity in schools was both inspiring and unwavering in equal measure.

Introduction

Creative Partnerships was a government-funded initiative put in place during 2001 by the Arts Council England. It operated across all nine English regions and it ran for a decade, closing in the summer of 2011. This book aims to draw on experiences from this programme, which was the largest creative education programme of its kind in the world. It will reflect on learning outcomes from this initiative, and is based on a unique body of research in order to provide points of reflection, and suggestions for embedding creative learning in any school and in any classroom.

The ambition to nurture creativity in young people through their experiences at school is an area of significant interest to educators and has been an important aspect of progressive, child-centred approaches to learning for many years. There has also been a good deal of interest at policy level over recent years, although there is much less consensus about what a 'creative education' might be in this regard. Is it about preparation for jobs in the creative industries? Is it about innovation and entrepreneurial skills? Is it just about good learning or is it about getting better results in exams? Is it about a set of habits or attributes that might be thought of as 'creative' and which might be fostered through particular pedagogical approaches? Might it be a blend of all of the above, and more?

Clearly, 'creativity' is a concept open to a wide variety of interpretations and is often used in a generic sense, rather than with precision. Particularly since the turn of the millennium, it has come to represent an important element within the basket of skills, behaviours and attitudes required to meet some of the pressing challenges that we, and the next generation, will face in the twenty-first century (Trilling and Fadel, 2009). The logic here is that since we cannot hope to predict the kinds of societies our children will grow up in or what jobs they might undertake as adults, the kinds of flexible, resilient and imaginative minds creative education develops could offer the best available preparation in our changing times.

Today, the ongoing challenges in the education sector are in fact a replay of long-standing debates about the purpose of schooling and the needs of young people (NACCCE, 1999). The frequent policy shifts and inflections – Creative Partnerships being just one example – often push and pull education between reform for fitness for contemporary and future societies, and a 'return' to an imagined educational high-point where the 'basics' were taught with greater rigour and the whole of society directly benefited as a result.[1] With such a loaded set of terms at its heart, and with a decades-old debate as yet unresolved still rumbling behind it, you might imagine that a national initiative such as Creative Partnerships would have struggled to make itself understood and that it might have fallen into the trap of being 'all things to all people'.

However, through careful planning and thanks to a network of dedicated professionals committed to connecting the worlds of the arts and creative practice with those of education and child development, this government-funded programme (2002–2011) not only managed to retain focus and coherence as it grew to work with over 5,000 schools, but also began to define more sharply, through applied practice in a wide variety of classrooms, some of the elusive concepts at the heart of creative work.

This book aims to set out and reflect on the main elements of the programme as they were seen through a number of research and evaluative projects, but rather than do so in a purely retrospective manner it attempts to extend an invitation to embed creative practice in schools to all teachers by offering a blend of thematic description and practical advice. Each chapter will look at a particular aspect of creative education and consider, from the perspective of the Creative Partnerships programme, what lessons might be drawn from the experience, what thinking points emerge that could inform practice in classrooms, and how the principles might be carried forward in schools not connected to a creative programme of any kind. It assumes no prior knowledge of Creative Partnerships and builds towards an essential set of transferable principles for any teacher or any school with ambitions to put creativity at the heart of their curriculum.

In this introduction I will briefly describe the Creative Partnerships programme; its roots in prior arts practice and various forms of progressive education, and the way it came to be structured and operated nationally. I will give a sense of how it transformed over time, from being a new policy idea to a programme and to something that could be applied day-to-day as sets of practices for teachers, artists and children. This will set the context for the main chapters that follow and it is hoped it will give the reader a clear understanding of the backstory that shapes the principles and themes explored later in the book.

What was Creative Partnerships and how did it work?

The government-funded initiative Creative Partnerships was an approach to working with schools that aimed to develop creativity in young people and improve their learning generally. It set out to achieve this by fostering partnerships between teachers and artists or other creative workers – from poets and dancers through to scientists and architects. The central hypothesis was that working and thinking practices in arts and creative professions would help unlock the full creative potential of teachers and their pupils. These partnerships would last for a significant period of time, typically between one and three years, sometimes longer. There was a leverage principle at the heart of the programme, namely, that through partnerships between the education sector and the arts and creative sector a richer learning yield might result. While teachers are already creative and flexible in many ways, it was thought that there were particular ways of thinking and working which were habitual to artists and other creative workers that might boost learning if they could be brought into schools in engaging ways. It was hoped that children would do better in terms of attainment, but would also develop the kinds of skills necessary for a rapidly shifting economic and social landscape. This was a response to a number of reports, for example, the report of the committee chaired by Sir Ken Robinson (NACCCE, 1999) and the DEMOS report, *The Creative Age* (1999), but also, and perhaps this is less-widely acknowledged, it was a broader sector-wide response to debates about the role and effectiveness of arts education and place of culture in the lives of young people. At the time, there was a growing sense that young people needed the chance to repeat arts and creative learning activities, rather than be offered a series of 'one-off' opportunities sometimes many months, or even years apart. In this sense, Creative Partnerships developed out of political will and an ongoing development of arts education.

Creative Partnerships was always a relatively well-funded initiative, but it began with modest numbers of schools, and from 2004 to 2011 it grew to be a very large programme indeed (see Appendix 1 for numbers of schools, teachers and young people who took part). In 2002, the initiative began in 16 areas across England[2] and each area was expected to work with between 15 and 20 schools. Many areas quickly moved on to work informally with more schools than this, often as a way of cementing relationships with Local Authorities and responding to varying levels of demand for the kinds of opportunities Creative Partnerships was offering. A second and third wave of Creative Partnerships areas were gradually introduced over 2004/5 and led to a total of 36 areas in all, four in each of the nine English regions.[3]

An intensive programme of research and evaluation helped the programme administrators, initially based within the Arts Council England, to understand the key elements of the programme. Over time, these insights led to a series of redefinitions of the approach, which in turn led to the formation of a revised Creative Partnerships programme in 2008. Key to this was the establishment of the role of 'creative agent', which will be explained below, and the creation of a network of independent delivery organisations, separate from the Arts Council England. At this stage the programme grew to reach larger numbers of schools through three programme strands – Enquiry Schools, Change Schools and Schools of Creativity.

All of this gives a flavour as to the size and spread of the programme and the pace of growth nationally. But what was actually happening in classrooms? The most effective Creative Partnerships work in schools was recognisable from the earliest days of the initiative. The challenge was how best to ensure that effective practice was happening in as many classrooms as possible. In order to do this it was important to reflect on how the most impactful projects were set up. But what did such work even look like in the schools?

Normally, a successful project would begin with some acknowledgement of the school's particular needs or pressing issues. Typically, this would reference back to the school's ongoing Improvement or Development Plan. By linking up with the long-term plans for the school, all the planning for Creative Partnerships activities would be relevant to the school's wider ambitions. From this basis, particular project ideas could be formed and would take their focus from the priority action areas for the school – it might be boys and literacy, developing outdoor learning spaces, developing questioning skills and risk-taking amongst teachers, or improving engagement and attendance amongst those pupils most disengaged from school. The list of focus areas for projects was as detailed and varied as school's individual sets of priorities and needs. It was not, by any means, a 'one-size-fits-all' programme.

With the project focus determined (and there might on average be two or three projects per year) the participants would begin a period of joint planning. Typically, this would involve teachers, artists and young people, overseen by a designated creative agent. The aim of the planning process was to be clear about roles, to set down expectations that were shared, understandable by all and which were felt to be achievable. During this phase the right kind of artist or creative worker would be matched to the school's needs, where the young people would get the opportunity to shape the experience they were about to embark upon and where the teacher could be clear about how the partnership with the artist(s) would be active, not passive. Planning in this way also allows for a shared definition of creativity to emerge, based on a framework provided by the programme, and for particular sorts of creative skill to be prioritised for development.

It is worth pausing here to describe the role of the creative agent in particular. Creative agents were professionals whose backgrounds were usually in the creative and cultural industries. As mentioned, schools to Creative Partnerships having already identified a specific issue or need that they would have liked the programme to help improve or develop. If the application was successful a creative agent would begin to work with school to extend the initial application. They worked in partnership with staff from senior teachers through to classroom assistants, helping to flesh out the early idea into a series of possible projects or programmes of work. From this more developed set of ideas the creative agent was able to work with schools to recruit the most appropriate creative practitioners who then worked with teachers and pupils on the projects.

Why was this seemingly protracted early process of planning and refining ideas actually needed, and why were creative agents required to play a role at this stage? We found that in the initial stages of a school's work it was vital to have a person in a position to be able to moderate the inevitable tensions that arose. These tensions occurred when a project based on principles of creative practice needed to be embedded within a school where the high level priorities for education, established nationally, had profoundly shaped the way the school operates and run counter to the kinds of creative values the school wants to develop for itself. Encouraging schools to identify the issues Creative Partnerships should focus on – which we did through a framework of evidence gathering called the Creative School Development Framework (CSDF)[4] – we felt we achieved a much higher level of engagement from school staff and they subsequently sought to embed changes in their practice long term. However, that level of commitment was something the creative agent was open about at the earliest stages and, in effect, it opened a Pandora's box of issues that were in fact points of tension between a centralised set of aims, and a localised set of needs. The creative agent was able to help keep these in balance.[5]

Additionally, schools in the programme seemed to us to require constructive challenge and support to help change occur. The creative agent was in a position to get to know the school and, in partnership with the teacher, to sensitively programme a series of projects that were constructed to suit the specific requirements and contexts that particular school had. This process, like the initial planning, is one that required a measure of balance and proportion – there must be attention to the character of the school and an acknowledgement of their unique 'start-line'; this is set against a programme of work that will create momentum and a move to a new way of doing things.

Later in this book we'll get a flavour of the kinds of projects that took place and the sorts of developments that arose from them, but for now it is enough to just keep in mind that the spine of the Creative Partnerships relationship with schools was based on the basic premise of an *initial audit of needs* and a phase of *joint planning*. We will also discuss in detail these important 'audit' and 'planning' phases and address the question of reflection and evaluation which was crucial to effective creative work.

What influenced Creative Partnerships?

Creative Partnerships was not a completely new idea. It was larger in scale and longer in duration than many prior arts-rich interventions in schools in England, but it drew, consciously or not, on a set of practices and histories developed through earlier work[6] and was staffed by people who in many cases felt that the programme encapsulated a good deal of what they were already doing.

However, as we shall see in later chapters, there were also times when perhaps the perceived fit between programme and pre-existing practices in the eyes of artists and teachers was not so neat. But at the outset it is important to note that in many respects the programme intuitively and implicitly drew inspiration and purpose from sets of loosely defined rhetorics.[7] Some of these were woven within policy and delivery agreements with government, others were manifest in the ways individual teachers and artists spoke about their approach and their intended outcomes with and for young people. As the programme developed it became evident that the most often asked question raised by people involved in the programme was: 'What do *you* mean by "creativity"?' As it is often unhelpful to have a fixed and single definition of a term that has such a wide range of interpretations and influences and so, rather than rule out the majority, we felt it was important to be explicit about as many 'takes' on creativity as we could. This would then allow everyone involved to explicitly orientate themselves in relation to one another's sense of what creativity was, to find a fit, or to keep looking for the right partners until a fit emerged. The first in a series of Creative Partnerships literature reviews focused on the multiple stances and meanings the term creativity (Banaji et al., 2006) and set out nine main claims made on behalf of the term. We found these to be a useful way of encouraging individuals to distinguish between types of creativity and to more explicitly locate themselves somewhere within these typologies. Reproduced from the review published by Creativity, Culture and Education, they are set out opposite (Reproduced from Banaji et al., 2010, pp. 69–71 with permission from CCE.)

1 **Creative genius**
   This is a post-romantic rhetoric that dismisses modernity and popular culture as vulgar, and argues for creativity as a special quality of a few individuals, either highly educated and disciplined, or inspired in some way, or both. Culture here is defined by a particular discourse about aesthetic judgment and value, manners, civilisation and the attempt to establish literary, artistic and musical canons. It can be traced back through certain aspects of the Romantic period to strands of European Enlightenment thought, in particular Kant's *Critique of Judgment*.

2 **Democratic and political creativity**
   This rhetoric provides an explicitly anti-elitist conceptualisation of creativity as inherent in the everyday cultural and symbolic practices of all human beings. It focuses particularly on the meanings made from and with popular cultural products. In its strongest formulations, it sees the creative work of young people as politically challenging. In one respect, it proceeds from empiricist traditions in which the material experiences of the individual in society lead to creative transformations. In an apparent contradiction, however, it also has roots in radical Romantic thinkers such as Blake, for whom children were agents of a revolutionary imagination, posing a political critique of church and state.

3 **Ubiquitous creativity**
   This entails the notion that creativity is not just about consumption and production of artistic products, whether popular or elite, but involves a skill in having the flexibility to respond to problems and changes in the modern world and one's personal life. While it is now commonly invoked alongside discussions of creativity as a social process and an ethical choice, the foundation of this rhetoric lies partly in early years education and the notion of providing young children with the tools to function successfully in the world.

4 **Creativity for social good**
   Seeing individual creativity as linked to social structures, this rhetoric is characterised by its emphasis on the importance for educational policy of the arts as tools for personal empowerment and ultimately for social regeneration. It stresses the integration of communities and individuals who have become 'socially excluded' (for example, by virtue of race, location or poverty) and invokes educational and economic concerns as the basis for generating policy interest in creativity. This rhetoric emerges largely from contemporary social democratic discourses of inclusion and multiculturalism.

5 **Creativity as economic imperative**
   The future of a competitive national economy is seen to depend, in this rhetoric, on the knowledge, flexibility, personal responsibility and problem-solving skills of workers and their managers. These are, apparently, fostered and encouraged

by creative methods in business, education and industry. There is a particular focus here on the contribution of the 'creative industries'. This rhetoric annexes the concept of creativity in the service of a neo-liberal economic programme and discourse.

6   **Play and creativity**
A persistent strand in writing about creativity, this rhetoric turns on the notion that childhood play is the origin of adult problem-solving and creative thought. It explores the functions of play in relation to both creative production and cultural consumption. Like aspects of the 'democratic' rhetoric, this notion of creativity as play, and its relation to education, emerges from strands of Romantic thought, in this case originating with Rousseau. There are important parallels between contemporary arguments for the role of creativity and the role of play in education.

7   **Creativity and cognition**
Ranging from theories of multiple intelligences and the testing of mental creativity levels, through explorations of the potential of artificial intelligence to demonstrate creative thought and production, to cultural psychology, this rhetoric frames creativity in psychological and scientific terms. Its emphasis at one extreme is on the internal production of creativity by the mind, and at the other extreme on external contexts and cultures. Its trajectory in education derives on the one hand from the Piagetian tradition; and on the other hand from the more culturally situated notions of creative learning expounded by Vygotsky, Dewey and Bruner.

8   **The creative affordances of technology**
If creativity is not inherent in human mental powers and is, in fact, social and situational, then technological developments may well be linked to advances in the creativity of individual users. This rhetoric covers a range of positions, from those who applaud all technology as inherently improving, to those who welcome it cautiously and see creativity as residing in an, as yet, under-theorised relationship between contexts, users and applications.

9   **The creative classroom**
Placing itself squarely at the heart of educational practice, this rhetoric focuses on connections between spirituality, knowledge, skills, creativity, teaching and learning and the place of creativity in an increasingly regulated and monitored curriculum. The focal point of this rhetoric is frequently practical advice to educators. This rhetoric locates itself in pragmatic accounts of 'the craft of the' classroom', rather than in academic theories of mind or culture.

While these rhetorics are explained in greater detail in the full literature review, they are summarised here to indicate how Creative Partnerships was interested in encouraging participants to clearly identify their own roots regarding creativity and to use the rhetorics as a means of more sharply delineating what 'type' of creativity participants are engaged in and committed to within their particular project. In this way, the categories act as a kind of filtration device for such a complex term. Of course, it is the case that they will often manifest themselves in varied combinations and arguably in ways that may contradict one another from time to time. Setting them out in explicit terms was one way the Creative Partnerships initiative aimed to promote a framework for debate rather than drift along with the assumption that we all meant the same thing by creativity all of the time. However, I do not want to suggest that these varied 'stances' are quite so neatly demarcated in the real world as they are in the list above. In the literature review, Banaji et al. (2010) provided useful prompt questions to promote this kind of debate; these are included in Appendix 2.

Creative Partnerships was also influenced by other initiatives, most recently the Arts Education Interface (AEI), a project based in Bristol and Corby that was described by the evaluators as comprising a 'mutual learning triangle' (Harland et al., 2005), a process of negotiated practice involving teachers, pupils and artists in arts-rich approaches to education. The evaluation warned against arts education being subsumed by 'creative and cultural education', which at the time was beginning to emerge as a policy concept. Additionally, it placed an emphasis on the importance of matching the right artistic skills with the particular learning needs of pupils rather than assuming that the 'arts' in a broader sense would indiscriminately add value to education. Both these ideas were current during the early development of Creative Partnerships, as we'll see in later chapters.

It is also worth noting that Creative Partnerships was a departure from the norm in as much as arts education and artists-in-schools programmes (which in general terms might be considered its precursor) received little attention from government since the advent of state education from 1870 onwards. The attention such work did receive was from the standpoint of arts as a palliative form of activity; it was a way of gaining some respite from the rigours of the curriculum 'proper' (Fleming, 2010, p. 23). Creative Partnerships was a departure from this view and, from the outset, focused on developing particular skills and enhancing curriculum attainment in a range of subject areas, not only the arts. In so doing it was, perhaps unknowingly, attempting to reconcile a series of post-war debates about the role and place of culture and creativity that revolved around three main beliefs, set out by Ken Jones:

1 a cultural conservatism for which tradition and authority are important reference points;
2 a progressivism concerned with child-centred learning;
3 and a tendency whose belief that 'culture is ordinary' [which] led to an insistence that working-class and popular culture should be represented in the classroom.

(Jones, 2009 p. 7)

Creative Partnerships was certainly drawing on these histories and philosophies tacitly but it was itself created at a particular moment in response to an emerging policy concern. So there was a strong political dimension to the programme. It was funded by two 'New Labour' government departments (the Department for Culture Media and Sport and the Department for Education) and was couched in a policy rhetoric which suggested it was both a means of boosting standards while being about more than just subject knowledge and a way of helping provide the sorts of skills necessary for the twenty-first century. A fuller account of the possibilities and tensions afforded by this kind of departmental joint-ownership of a programme is explored more fully elsewhere (Parker and Ruthra-Rajan, 2011, pp. 448–458) but for now it is enough to note that while Creative Partnerships was generously funded as a programme, and had very strong initial support within government, it was also borne of a long a complex history and professional practices and was subject to the usual agendas that come to the fore in any large-scale programme looking to change ways of teaching in school.

Initially, navigating through this terrain was the task of teams of Creative Partnerships staff, national and local, employed by the Arts Council England. Then, from 2009 onwards, it became the responsibility of Creativity, Culture and Education (CCE), which continued to manage the programme once the Arts Council England had let it go. There was a high level of continuity of staff between both phases. The experiences and learning developed through the time CCE were custodians of the Creative Partnerships form the substance of the chapters that follow.

Notes

1   http://www.independent.co.uk/news/education/education-news/outcry-as-michael-gove-issues-education-reform-warning–7274827.html

2   Phase 1 – began 2002: Cornwall, Bristol, London East, London South, Norfolk, Nottingham, Birmingham, Manchester/Salford, Durham/Sunderland, Tees Valley, Merseyside, Black Country, Kent, Slough, Hull and Barnsley, Doncaster and Rotherham.
Phase 2 – began 2004: Coventry, Derby, London North, Southampton/Isle of Wight, Plymouth, North/South Tyneside, Cumbria, Bradford, Basildon.
Phase 3 – began 2005: Thurrock, Tendring, Bolsover, Ashfield and Mansfield, Leicester, East Lancashire, London West, Northumberland, Hastings and East Sussex, Forest of Dean, Stoke-on-Trent and Sheffield.

3   East, East Midlands, London, North East, North West, South East, South West, West Midlands and Yorkshire and Humber.

4   For an analysis of a sample of completed CSDFs see the 'Synoptic Survey' undertaken by David Wood Consultants: *Creative Partnerships, Change School Programme Synoptic Evaluation* (2011).

5   The genesis of the Creative School Development Framework lay in work and development by Chris May, director of Creative Partnerships East Lancashire. Chris was keen to understand for himself, and to be able to reflect back to participating schools, internal perceptions on strengths, weaknesses and overall capacity to take on the challenges of setting up a programme of creative learning.

6   The most recent initiative that fed into the development of Creative Partnerships was the Arts Education Interface (AEI) (Harland, *et al.* 2005). But there were a range of other policies and initiatives that influenced Creative Partnerships in more subtle ways. Education Action Zones, which emerged in the late 1990s (Ofsted, 2001), for example, with their focus on regeneration and 'reaching the hardest to reach' showed how a range of social benefits might be fostered by innovative education work. The All Our Futures report (1999) was composed in part to help refine the national curriculum, a process led by the Qualifications and Curriculum Authority, and in contrast to earlier reports, particularly the Gulbenkian report (1982). All Our Futures foregrounded the role of the arts in advancing learning across all subjects, not just those with overt arts content. Earlier policies that influenced the education ecology Creative Partnerships was set up to service also include the Plowden Report (1967) with its focus on child-centred progressivism. Although it is also interesting to reflect that the strong

focus on self-expression within this report arguably created a swing back to a sense of a 'core curriculum'. A division between expression and learning "the basics" endures to this day.

7 My use of the term 'rhetorics' borrows from Banaji *et al.* (2006) and refers to a series of different 'claims' made for creativity each of which develops out of a distinct philosophical, political, educational and/or psychological position.

1 Creative Planning and Evaluating – Change Processes or Change Arts Projects?

This chapter provides a summary of how Creative Partnerships set about assessing start points for participating schools. There were particular systems we used which helped guide the thinking of all those people involved in making the work happen in classrooms and they will be described here. This chapter will show how it is important to give some thought about the kinds of expertise and the sorts of value creative partners might add when working in partnership with teachers.

Partnerships in any line of work can be immensely productive, bringing additional resources and expertise to bear on a given task; but it would also be true to say partnerships can increase the chances of confusion or misinterpretation. By definition, with a multiplication of viewpoints and agendas, there is an increased need to understand what work is to be embarked on, to understand it from a range of perspectives, to be clear why it is better to do it as a collaboration, and what the particular skills and advantages each partner might bring to achieve the desired outcome. At times, it might be best to be flexible about the ways to achieve the particular outcome. But whatever the agreed activities, and whatever the intended outcomes are understood to be, they should be shared and roles should be clear. In essence, to successfully work in partnership we are faced with a choice: we can carry sets of assumptions and hope they are not going to be exposed down the line or we can ask questions of one another up front and establish clear roles and open communication from the outset. Yet, this also raises several questions. Why is it better that we embark upon this work together, rather than apart? And what do we get out of it? Are they the same benefits or different altogether?

Creative Partnerships could only work effectively when these basic questions were first addressed. This can be a surprise for people who feel that creativity is all about improvisation and nothing to do with planning. In this case, in our experience, it is better to go to the trouble to set out initial thoughts and expectations for everyone involved, even if they may change and deviate later. In this chapter, I want to describe how in the Creative Partnerships programme, we set about building partnerships by going through a staged process of asking key questions, and I want to explain why this was such an important thing to do. I will summarise the key principles and set out a broad framework so that you can take a similar approach in your own educational setting.

Questions, questions, questions

Of course creativity is very much about spontaneity, fun and improvisation. So having to pause at the very early stages of a project to set out what you might want to achieve might seem contradictory. A common question is why the need for all this planning if we find ourselves veering off course quite naturally soon after we begin?

There are a number of reasons why building a foundation through initial questioning and planning is a good thing but above all else, having some kind of initial reference point to reflect back on is a great aid to evaluation. It was for this reason that within Creative Partnerships, planning and evaluation were strongly linked.

Why evaluate anyway?

Evaluation is often used as a summative activity to describe a project, regardless of its quality, after the event. In other words, it is a mechanism for simply reporting that something happened, usually because it was paid for by an organisation that must account for the distribution of funds. Many of us have probably used evaluation in this way as part of our professional lives at some point, but in so doing it is easy to neglect the on-going critique that is actually key to developing and improving practice while a project is still 'live'. Good evaluation systems that encourage on-going critical reflection are best not thought of as historical documents, but rather as tools for ensuring that the activity we do is of quality, has focus, is rigorous and can offer findings that help us all improve in our work quickly with an explanation of why and how this is the case. In other words, if evaluation is not interwoven with project or lesson management it probably isn't working as well as it could.

The Creative Partnerships approach to planning and evaluation approach aimed to offer evidence that might be used in final reports, but much more importantly, it aspired to give all those participating in a project the kind of feedback they might use to fine tune projects while they were still in progress. So how was the Creative Partnerships approach devised?

What was required was a model that could systematically assess if, and how, children, teachers, schools and practitioners were changing and being changed by the process of creative learning through cultural practice. At the time, no model existed that was appropriate to our needs and as a result, a fresh way of assessing creative learning was developed and put in to practice. After several years of application and refinement the final Creative Partnerships evaluation model is still being used in new programmes at the time of writing and promises to offer teacher-friendly tools by which to assess the progression of creative habits and skills.

When it was first developed, the evaluation worked as a set of distinct phases over the lifetime of a project, be it a week or a year, and was used to facilitate the evaluation process in a manageable and productive way.

The first version of the Creative Partnerships evaluation model was generated not simply from our own field research and observations, but from a range of academic sources that I will set out below.

The overview offered by Cropley (2001) in Creativity in Education and Learning, in particular his synthesis of the properties of a creative person (pp. 124 and 148), offered a starting point for the evaluation approach that Creative Partnerships developed. We began by exploring the properties set out by Cropley in the approach taken by practitioners, teachers and young people in the classroom, to see if they emerged through Creative Partnerships practice. Many of these features were noted, but when we looked across a significant number of projects some appeared more prevalent than others. The Creative Partnerships area that really led the development of this model was Kent, and much of the energy and thought required to get the evaluation approach off the ground was due to the then Director of Creative Partnerships, Anna Cutler. When Creative Partnerships first began research, commissioned by Cutler, it 'showed that these recurrent features could possibly be learned rather than be considered innate personal qualities. Anna Cutler also commissioned research that began to deconstruct the 'properties' to reveal the kinds of practice that generates such creative features (Blunt, 2004). These practices were then further distilled to arrive at a smaller number of core recurrent features in Creative Partnerships work.

The work of Anna Cutler and her team in Creative Partnerships, Kent, did most to bring form and clarity to the evaluation approach through ongoing practical assessments of projects. However, there were also several key texts and schools of thought that helped develop the approach to evaluation adopted by all Creative Partnerships areas from 2005 onwards. Ken Robinson's *Out of Our Minds* (2001) and Richard Florida's *The Rise of the Creative Class* helped give a shape for a broader context of the features of creativity in the twenty-first century, whilst practice already available such as that of Reggio Emilia and Steve Seidal's *Making Learning Visible*, Children *as*

Individual and Group Learners was informative in terms of the detail of what ongoing practice we needed to observe and record in any evaluation model.

The work of Shirley Brice Heath, *Ways with Words, Visual Learning in the Community School* and *Made for Each Other* (the latter two co-authored with Shelby Wolf and Elke Paul Boekne respectively) were highly influential in understanding the importance of language input and impacts in creativity. Extended discussions with Heath on organisational learning and creative practice also helped shape Creative Partnerships' understanding of the core features of creative learning through the arts.

Tom Bentley and Kimberley Seltzer's *The Creative Age* (1999) informed and distilled several definitions and ideas around aspects of creativity itself and the methods of approach (see also Learning Beyond the Classroom, Assessment in Context page 144). *The Creative Age* introduces creativity as something that can be learned and that it is not an individual characteristic or innate talent but that: 'creativity is the application of knowledge and skills in new ways to achieve a valued goal.' (p. 10). This understanding is one that was supported by our own observations and we hope, is reflected in our model. Similar ideas are also apparent in Ken Robinson's definition offered in *Out of Our Minds* as well as the Qualifications and Curriculum Authority's (formerly QCA, currently known as the Qualifications and Curriculum Development Agency) document *Creativity: Find it, Promote i*t, though each come with distinct perspectives.

There are many other sources that were drawn upon such as the work of CAPE (Chicago Arts Partnership in Education), and Professor Anna Craft, but those mentioned above were the key influences used to set up the evaluation structure and method of approach that resulted in the initial evaluation approach used by Creative Partnerships: a four phase evaluation model. This model has been designed to be used specifically to evaluate work based on partnership principles – it attempts to get a feel for the contributions of all participants and changes and impacts that occur for them as a result. However, it also offers a good breakdown of how to think about the sorts of inputs required if you are planning for creative learning within a project, or as way of teaching across a range of curriculum subjects.

The four phase evaluation model

This evaluation process will provide:

- Identifiable features of creative learning to look for within a project.

- A planning tool for your project or scheme of work relevant to the particularities of creativity.
- The basis of a common language with which to discuss creative learning with other teachers, practitioners and pupils.[1]
- A basic analysis of what helps to generate change.
- The ability to compare across effects of very different projects – i.e. different arts or creative practices that are united by common principles at the level of input
- Information for the purposes of monitoring if required.
- Data that is both quantitative and qualitative.
- Evidence of what works and why.
- Evidence of what doesn't work and why.
- A measurement of how things have changed.
- Confidence to articulate your observations coherently.
- The identification of anomalies that may require further detailed research.
- Patterns that indicate important features about creative learning.
- A better knowledge and understanding of the creative work you are undertaking with pupils.
- A structured, manageable and flexible system for monitoring all creative learning lessons or projects.
- Quality assurance and reasons to reject a project idea or revise it.
- For an initial investment of time and thought, more time saved down the line by better delivery and outcomes.

Four phase progression

Figure 1.1 represents the four phases of a self-evaluation process: Input, Doing, Showing and Reflection. This diagram, in its original form, was the basis of training and workshops led and devised by Anna Cutler and the idea is developed further in an article for the Tate (Cutler, 2010). The features in each phase have been carefully selected from the literature and experience from the Creative Partnerships programme as crucial aspects key to creative learning. Each phase will be defined and its terms will be identified and explained.

Phase 1: Input

Early observations within the Creative Partnerships programme suggested that there were five 'inputs' that were most noted and apparent in successful creative learning

Four Phase Progression

1. Input
Idea
Language
Environment
Resources
Qualities and values

2. Doing
Identifying problems
Divergent thinking
Co-learning
Fascination
Risk-taking
Skills and challenges
Refinement

4. Reflection
What has changed for the
school, the practitioner and
the young people? In terms of:
Input (all features)
Doing (all features)
Showing (all features)

Unexpected outcomes?

3. Showing
Solving problems
New ideas
Capacity to learn
Engagement
Confidence
New skills
Purposeful
Learning/outcomes

Figure 1.1 Creative Partnerships Four Phase Progression Model of Evaluation

practices and projects. These were: the quality of ideas, the use of language, the challenge to the known environment and the quality of the resources as well as the qualities and values of the practitioner. Each of these are examined in detail below. These elements are worth prioritising in your own planning for lessons and projects.

In Creative Partnerships the Input phase related to the different ways of working, thinking and doing of the individual, team or organisation that was entering the education environment. An easy shorthand term might be 'added value': what are the particular aspects of your project, scheme of work or lesson that was new or different in some way to the usual environment and that would otherwise not exist? Asking such questions early on gets teachers, artists and if possible young people thinking about what sorts of skills or processes they might draw upon to enrich their learning. It is important to ask the questions straightforwardly and of course, to answer honestly. If there is no perceived added value of an individual or organisation going in to a school, if there will be no real difference to the way things are already happening, it is worth rethinking the general premise of the project. It is far better to realise this at an early stage, than much later down the line. Of course, it would be possible consider this phase without creative practitioners coming in as external partners, but if you are attempting to develop teaching in creative ways and do so without recourse to partnerships with artists and others, the early questions might revolve around how the teaching staff are consciously planning to do things differently – new ways of teaching and assessing, mobilising new resources, using different vocabularies and terminologies for example – to the exclusion of the artists and creative practitioners.

The five inputs identified by Creative Partnerships were:

- **Idea.** This involves conceptual quality, scale and originality of the idea developed for the project, (and, if appropriate, with particular reference to the part played by the creative practitioner in developing the idea whilst understanding that ideas are often generated by the young people and teachers too). Is the concept at the heart of the project different to the norm, is there scope for it to offer learners opportunities to improvise and take risks, to take on ownership of the idea? Many schools are expert at offering very focused curriculum-linked ideas for projects, and are used to working along these lines. Such ideas might be incorporated too, but if at the early stage the idea is too tightly focused, too linked to targets and levels, recognisable as the kind of learning already at the heart of pedagogy in the school, and if an external partner is expected to simply 'deliver' it differently, then based on the experience of Creative Partnerships, it is time to rethink. This is because, in essence, it situates the creative element to the side, or treats it as something to be bolted on, rather than a way of fundamentally reframing the learning journey.

- **Language.** This refers to the use of professional language introduced by the practitioner as well as the way in which they speak to children/educational staff and others. This was a crucial aspect in the Creative Partnerships programme as external partners often bring with them a new vocabulary and discourse, and powerful ways to unlock creative behaviours of children. Language does not simply refer the ways in which creative practitioners have a set of different technical terminologies to describe their work, but it is also the ways in which they use language in modes that admit emotion to a greater degree. Not to generalise but they will often talk in the first person, which may seem a banal point, but is often a stark contrast to the ways educators have been encouraged to remain impersonal and detached in the classroom. Of course there will be exceptions to this, but it was a feature we noted across the whole of the Creative Partnerships initiative and it will be alluded to often in the chapters to come, particularly those focused on ethos, well-being and the unique approach taken by creative practitioners.

- **Environment.** This refers to the way(s) in which the usual learning environment is changed or challenged by the practitioner/project. Although schools in England are often expected to respond to a whole raft of agendas, from children's health, parental engagement, through to attainment in core subjects, and the fact that the inspection system is continually looking for improvement, there are still many stable features within school and the environment is often the most fixed of these. The way classroom spaces are used physically and the way outdoor areas are designed to stimulate learning, are often underwhelming and indeed unchanged for decades in many cases, while technical kit such as computers are upgraded, or whiteboards installed. Creative learning often begins by taking a fresh look at the learning environment, indoors and out, and can offer a fresh perspective on how to make use of the environment that go back to first principles.

- **Resources.** This refers to any new materials taken in to the educational environment and their quality/appropriateness when considered in relation to those usually found in the educational environment. This might be new technical equipment, or different sorts of pens or brushes, or a new use for existing equipment that reveals a hidden potential. Again, this is of particular interest when creative practitioners are working on projects as they draw on repertoires of skill and experience that often bring teachers and students into contact with new materials or artefacts that have a different quality about them.

- **Qualities and values [of the practitioners].** Before a project begins, if you are planning on working with an external partner, it is worth reflecting on what kinds of values and qualities such a partner brings when they go in to a school and whether it is possible to have particular sorts of quality and value in mind when choosing a project partner. If you are not working with an external artist, this would be an opportunity to reflect on your own qualities and values. Sometimes gender is a key issue, at other times age or ethnicity. It may simply be that the challenging nature of the individual is the important factor – what in Creative Partnerships was often spoken of as the 'grit in the oyster' – that key added ingredient that helps something extra special occur.

The way these different elements work within the self-evaluation process is as follows:

- Inputs can be given a value BEFORE the creative work starts in full (this may be after a practitioner has been working to devise a programme with staff and students)
- Inputs can then be given a value DURING the work if long-term (certainly it should be work that is more sustained than a day session and if lasting change is to be developed, the longer the better)
- And inputs can be given a value AFTER the project, when the sessions/lessons/workshops have been completed.

In the Creative Partnerships programme we asked participants to give their values at each stage using a 0–3 scale for each aspect. The forms used to do this during the first year of using this model are in Appendix 4.

If you are working with an external partner, then the practitioner (the external organisation/individual) and the school (usually the class teacher involved) are asked to do this individually (this is more time-consuming, but we found people to be more candid when reflecting on these matters separately than when together, and this made for more interesting points of learning after the programmes of work). We ask the staff and practitioners to discuss this with the young people, covering each aspect in an appropriate way. Clearly this will depend on age and the nature of the projects taking place.

If the values score less than 2 from the outset, it throws into question the expected quality and purpose of the project. Since this process of evaluation has built into it joint planning for the project we are not being asked to consider, 'how do you think you'll feel about x or y?', which may lead to sets of low expectations for all sorts of valid reasons, including disappointment from past experiences. Instead, we are asking people to say how they want it to be, and to take an active role in shaping that process. The partnership element is key here. If all participants are not looking to generate something between them that has a high expected value, why should we expect the work to have any significant impact on creativity or learning?

Phase 2: Doing

After extensive reading and observation of practice, seven features of creativity in learning situations were selected as the most frequently recurring and necessary aspects required for creative learning to take place. These features were important in establishing high quality Creative Partnerships practice and may be useful to bear in mind whether working in partnership with an external provider or planning a series lessons with other teachers.

This phase relates to the experience of the project for young people, practitioners and teachers while it is 'live', i.e. being delivered in school. The seven features of creative learning are outlined below.

- **Identifying problems.** Does proposed work seek to challenge any issues? How will it promote questioning and problem finding? What kinds of problems might the project focus on and will this be an important part of the experience for everyone? Examples may be as diverse as bullying in a school, the low level of boys' language development in Year 1, or students trying out lots of different approaches to find a 'way in' to learning a particular concept. Projects that encourage problem identification are important if we have ambitions for young people to also develop problem-solving skills. Both are key aspects of creative learning.

- **Divergent thinking.** This relates to the ways the project offers opportunities for different and original ways of thinking, and admits different perspectives. It also covers the notion of a plurality of ideas and possibilities within a project, that they might be generated and made use of and chances to make novel use of the imagination. It also refers to experiences that allow unusual elements/ideas to be put together in new configurations and allow people to test them out. Creative learning creates the climate for such thinking and this is a chance to consider the extent to which the project is offering ways of doing this. If the project is failing to do this, and there may be good reasons for it, it is a chance to be explicit about what those reasons are.

- **Co-learning.** This refers to the ways creative practitioners work with the students and staff in a situation where all participants are learning something new together, or where teachers are learning with the pupils in respect of skills or specific knowledge the practitioners share. Creative learning (and characteristic of many artists' approaches to working with young people) is often about being the 'guide on the side' not the 'sage on the stage'. (Galton, 2012) 'Co-learning' is a process that can 'flatten' hierarchical relationships and can link back to the ways language is used and the way the environment is set up. Our hypothesis was that creative practitioners would bring practices that encouraged co-learning, and established conditions whereby this mode of learning became productive and comfortable for all involved.

- **Fascination.** This term focuses on the degree of engagement and interest shown by those involved and how this might be generated by the activity (for example, by explicitly planning for preferred learning styles). It is worth noting whether fascination in your project is sustained beyond the project hours. Much anecdotal evidence of the effectiveness of Creative Partnerships projects centred on this sense of new found fascination in participants, an almost irrepressible need to model inquisitive behaviours in other lessons, or other areas of life, or a desire to explore something new long after the project had ended. Creative learning engages the individual in rewarding activities that stimulate a deep motivation and persistent interest. It is important to consider whether your project offers an opportunity for this to happen.

- **Risk-taking.** Risk-taking here is intended to indicate the degree to which participants are able to move beyond their comfort zones, to take a chance and to be prepared to fail – all within the spirit of finding things out and exploring alternatives. 'High stakes' risks, which sometimes inspire a sense of nervousness – a performance or a final product – while not being an over-dominating end in itself, can be important. These public performances or events can be an effective vehicle for creative opportunities to achieve a valued and communicable goal and to create emotional engagement. However, what counts as 'risk' for people is relative. As we will see, for example, in the chapter dealing with parental engagement, for many in Creative Partnerships seemingly small changes of viewpoint or steps towards trying new pastimes or activities were often seen as big risks. One of the skills of schools and artists within Creative Partnerships was to effectively create a mixture of activities, sometimes offering low-risk 'invitations' which initially were calibrated up over time to help people feel less and less uncomfortable about the notion of risk in learning and thereby developing a willingness to try something new.

- **Skills and challenges.** This aspect relates to the balance between skills and new challenges. Does the project effectively use the skills of those involved and stretch them? Or are they kept within the limits of what they can already do? Are they thrown too quickly into a complex new challenge without adequate resources to get themselves through it? In terms of educational theory it might be thought of as analogous to the notion of scaffolding, creating a designed and planned for degree of extension and growth that helps learners to use known skills, acquire some new knowledge in the process, and in some respects meet the challenge set.

- **Refinement.** This refers to the discipline of practice, repetition and fine-tuning in creative work and creative learning. Creative Partnerships projects attempted to give people the opportunity to get better at something by trying it out and refining their process, through repeated opportunities, over an extended period of time. While it was not the only programme to try to do this, it was comparatively rare in the arts and cultural sector where shorter-term work has tended to be the norm. Does your learning opportunity provide chances to do this? Will you have the opportunity to have more than one run at something? Are you prepared for some attempts to fail, and for that to be positively encouraged as a purposeful creative act?

As part of the Creative Partnerships programme, sometimes during and occasionally soon after a project had finished (depending on logistics and availability of all involved), a series of brief questionnaires was sent out to schools and to practitioners to ask them to identify, on a scale of 0–3, if and how exactly the project incorporated the features of creative learning as described above and to what extent this seemed to be a change from their usual mode of learning.

Questionnaires were often not used with children in classrooms. In many instances an alternative format was devised for collecting information from young people, activities that generated responses in keeping with the broad categories above. A notebook in the style of a reflective journal to capture viewpoints and evidence was often found to be useful by teachers and artists. Very often artists and other creative professionals made regular use of such journals anyway, and were able to offer insights into ways such journals might be set up and made use of in reflective practice.

Phase 3: Showing

These aspects of what we thought of as the 'Showing' phase in a creative learning experience relate back to most of the objectives relevant to children and teachers that are delivered during the prior 'Doing' phase. This also includes the impacts that the experience has on the children, for example, increasing confidence.

- **Solving problems.** This relates back to 'Identifying problems' in the Doing phase, but here in the Showing phase we want to be able to point to evidence that this has happened for learners. Namely, the ability, having identified a problem for oneself, to resolve it to one's own, and others' satisfaction and be able to move forwards.
- **New ideas.** Originality is a very difficult concept for creative learning to wrestle with. There is always the debate as to what 'original' and 'new' mean in the context of learning – does it mean novel to those involved and new for the context they happen to be in, or new to the world? In Creative Partnerships, it was generally the case that originality considered as the kind of novelty that was confined to specific situations and groups of people, although there were some projects that were strikingly original and sufficiently large in scale to grab media attention.[2]

  This aspect also indicates the capacity for learners to offer up new ideas in learning situations. It is a sign that learning is considered a process of generation as much as one of reception – so that as well as fact-finding and knowledge transmission, one might also expect to find a growing ability to explore, discover and test out the plausibility of concept through the creation of new ideas. This may also be manifest through, for example, inventive language, drawing or dance.
- **Capacity for learning.** This refers to the ways in which participants' ability to learn and overall interest in learning is manifest. Have dispositions towards learning become more positive? Is there a need among learners to follow up on activities? Is there spillover from interest in one subject to others, or after school activities? Are learners making links and connections between subjects more often? Is the appetite for learning growing in such a way as to be self-sustaining beyond the classroom?

- **Engagement.** Following on from 'Fascination' in the previous phase, this aspect refers to the strength and depth of involvement in a project or programme. This is often manifest through, for example, improved attendance, where children stay later to finish off tasks or even simply show a desire to do so; taking on supplementary tasks to enrich the main work of the project and the learning related to it; or committing to developing some aspect of the skills or aptitudes developed in school through an out-of-school pursuit of some kind.

- **Confidence.** One of the most important, and often one of the earliest impacts of creative work with young people is a growth in confidence. In Creative Partnerships we took this to be the capacity to have self-belief, and to be able to share this with others. The opportunity to take risks in the prior phase of the project was often a strong predictor for learners developing a more confident approach to learning and presenting their own understanding back to groups or audiences.

- **New skills.** New skills developed for those involved are frequently a direct result of the project. These might be particular sorts of creative skills (Creativity Culture and Education (CCE) has commissioned a research project, still ongoing at the time of writing, which seeks to build a model of learning progression and assessment just around creative skills and behaviours and this will feature in Chapter 8). They might also be arts skills or the acquisition of knowledge in specific curriculum areas. For teachers, too, this is an interesting aspect to reflect on in terms of teaching skills and might include the development of a broader repertoire of approaches to teaching and learning, the experience of partnership working, from joint-planning through to shared reflection and an ability to more sharply define the needs of the school and the learner and how that might be matched by the affordances and specific capacities of the creative and cultural sector.

- **Purposeful learning/outcomes.** As well as the skills developed, creative and otherwise, there will often be some targeted aspect of curriculum-based learning that is worthwhile keeping track of so that you can assess the impact of the project in this. This might be subject-based knowledge and skills, or the kinds of meta-cognitive skills that overlap with individual creative skills that we will come on to consider in Chapter 8. It might also include unexpected by-products that emerge from the project and which can be noted here – all those unexpected outcomes that may be surprising, but still have a clear purpose and are of value. These may range from a shift in classroom discourse, an increase in the use of open-ended questioning, or a new inclusive language of learning where the teacher refers back to their own development explicitly, through to the SATs results improving or children developing an awareness that their learning needs are the most significant aspect in learning, leading to changed teaching practice.

As part of the Creative Partnerships programme, as a way of marking participant's perceptions during this phase, both during and sometimes soon after a project had completed, a series of questionnaires were sent out to schools and practitioners to ask them to identify on a scale of 0–3 the extent to which the project enabled the above features of creative learning phases and whether this was felt to be a change from the norm. As previously stated, a questionnaire would not necessarily be appropriate to gather evidence in an individual school or classroom. But a format for logging and referring back to the aspects outlined above, as the basis for reflection and learning can be a very useful thing – be it using journals or notebooks, comment-boards and photos to document learning. The way the comments look is not as important as the fact that they are anchored to the aspects and principles outlined above. You must be inventive in your approach and devise fit-for-purpose mechanisms for discussion and notation. You should be genuinely reflective in practice, welcoming of different viewpoints and use difference and commonality equally, as points of learning and joint reflection. It is a rewarding process, but it does require a significant commitment and a good deal of effort.

Phase 4: Reflection

This phase relates not only to a reflection of the whole experience, a consideration of how things might be planned and delivered differently next time, but also to meta-cognition: understanding how we know what we know about the experience of creative learning. This often involves application of any unexpected outcomes in the next phase of activity.

By reflection we refer to a process of critique and consideration as to the quality and impact of creative learning, motivated by the desire to build a culture of improvement and development in relation to this approach to education. While CCE was aware of and very much appreciated the opportunity this phase of a project offered participants to celebrate, to persuade, to report back to a range of interested constituencies (Local Authority contacts, governing bodies, parents and others) about the benefits of creative practice, we wanted to emphasise that these things were important by-products of a more objective assessment about the overall quality of the project and a longer-term reflective process about learning that was hoped to build some commitment to. This approach to planning and evaluation was always intended to be a recursive experience of deep reflection followed the re-application of practice in classrooms. This may well be a CCE-inflected description of a mode of reflection already well known to committed teachers and widely practised by them. There is no intention to suggest otherwise. However, it was anecdotally reported by many involved in the Creative Partnerships programme that the novelty of the projects, the fun nature of many of the activities, or, to borrow a term from Anne Bamford, the 'Wow Factor' they seemed to carry with them, sometimes led people to take a perspective of uncritical celebration of the outcomes rather than to reflect on specific reasons why they might have occurred. It is worth guarding against the temptation to collude in a belief that things always went smoothly, or the outcomes were always positive, even if the motives for so doing are based on the desire to advocate the principles of creative learning.

Participants in creative projects or lessons will generate examples that relate back to aspects in both the 'doing' and 'showing' phases in varied ways throughout every project. The reality is often a very rich, fast-paced, often quite messy process so it takes some skill to notice, capture, disaggregate and reflect on significant elements every time the project takes place. But it is possible, and in our experience it is richly rewarding.

'Ways in' with planning and evaluation

Getting started

There are a number of good ways to begin working with this approach to evaluating creative projects. One is to distribute hypothetical projects amongst your peers and then go through the evaluation from start to finish, interviewing each other. This was an approach used very effectively in the Creative Partnerships Kent area, in the South-East region of England. This approach builds a collective understanding of the process and the terms involved and what may or may not stand as good evidence of effects.

Another way in for groups looking to develop this approach is to undertake a 'big paper exercise'. This involves securing large sheets of flip chart paper on a wall around a room or on tables. The key is to set out the sheets in such a way that the group can circulate and write on them comfortably. For each of the creative aspects in the Input, Doing and Showing phases, invite all members of the group to write a one-line definition of that aspect. Do not discourage people from reading one another's work, but also suggest that there is no need for them to be particularly 'led' by definitions that are already emerging if they feel a different one is more appropriate. When this is completed the list generated under each heading should prove to be a good discussion point, and from our experience of Creative Partnerships, there tends to be a good deal of consensus about each term. This also builds a strong collective sense of what is meant by these terms and stands the group in good stead for evaluating the creative work when it happens in classrooms.

Capturing the information

As part of the Creative Partnerships programme we used a creative learning Record Sheet (Appendix 4) and this gave a clear indication of what to ask and a key to the value to be assigned to each aspect of the project. (0=no value 1=some value 2=good value and 3=significant value.)

Of course, you may have better ways to capture this information but the main thing is to keep the features of each stage outlined above in focus and to tie discussions and evidence back to them.

The 0–3 values were not designed by Creative Partnerships to be a proper metric where one might infer empirical shifts toward creativity in schools, they were intended to serve more as a general indicator of the overall direction of the project. It was another way of helping to promote discussion, to avoid a lowest-common denominator agreement or unconscious 'fence-sitting'. It was always useful to have genuine differences of opinion aired and discussed as this generated learning and reflection. The numerical values were useful as a formative tool, a device for signalling where and what was needed next. Final project values were always considered with interest, but we kept in mind that there would be varied interpretations of the facets in the planning, doing and showing stages across all of the Creative Partnerships projects borne of a necessary subjectivism that resisted national aggregation.

If you are an individual teacher trying out creative approaches to teaching and learning, you may decide not to use sheets, since there may be other tools more suited to your needs. Some teachers, artists and children kept a project log, an annotated notebook, journal or some other similar format that allowed them to note and capture comments while continuing to move on with the project. In our view it is advisable to structure any journal you use along the lines of the phases and creative aspects as shown in the model described above, rather than keep a series of diary entries which will require more time to organise and categorise down the line.

Ultimately, the net you use to capture the evidence is as varied as your own needs and preferences; the important point of commonality is that the features we are looking to catch in the net, and the evidence that stands for each, are broadly similar in quality and in definition.

Making sense of it all

Evaluation demands judgement. There is no point collecting evidence and reflections unless they will be put to use, and in the case of creative projects this will always involve judgements as to value. Whether you have used questionnaires, semi-structured conversations and/or your own observations and notes about how a project is developing, this rich material puts you in a very strong position to make informed calls about the value and suitability of particular approaches for your pupils. Just collating the information without analysing it will give you or, more importantly, those wanting to understand and build on what you've done, a descriptive record of what happened without any reasoned thoughts as to why.

Here are some examples of questions that may need to be answered through analysis of the evidence you using your preferred process.

- Which projects or series of lessons 'scored' the highest and why?
- Are there common features of all the projects that seem to be most successful?
- Which projects scored the lowest and why?
- Does this make them a poorly planned project or is there something positively challenging about them that prompts, in a sense, a 'false negative' score?
- Are there common features in those that scored the lowest?
- Do the Inputs for the most successful projects also score highly?
- What kinds of practitioners or practices are gaining the highest score in the input and why?
- Are there any anomalies, what are these and why do you think they are occurring?
- Do the children's responses echo those of the teachers and practitioners; is there any reason why, or why not?
- What types of projects seem to be achieving most change in primary schools?
- What types of projects seem to be achieving most change in secondary schools?
- Are there any diversity issues that impact on the quality of input?
- What kinds of projects seem to best improve behaviour/attendance/communication?

Examples of noteworthy aspects of this model of planning and evaluating

In the Creative Partnerships programme we found some aspects of this model of planning and evaluating more valuable than others. Some examples of these are outlined below.

Identifying problems/solving problems

The ability to identify and solve problems, we found, required space for more questions and additional time for thinking independently. It also involved a process of 'showing one's workings', whereby participants gave reasons for judgements when making decisions. The broad observation here is that if we want children to be better at solving problems we first need to give them the opportunity to ask lots of questions with confidence. When planning for projects, lessons or workshops it is important to build in such opportunities.

Divergent thinking/new ideas

We noted that the development of divergent thinking skills seemed to be fuelled by a rich supply of new information, fresh stimuli, opportunities to make connections and a freedom to things to try out and be prepared for these 'try outs' to sometimes fail. This worked well when there was adequate space and time to properly explore alternatives. It is worth keeping in mind that projects that incorporate the opportunity to be stimulated by new experiences and new knowledge can lead to this outcome and to plan accordingly.

Co-learning/capacity to learn

We observed that co-learning appeared to offer a positive shared experience for adults and young people alike. Many participants suggested that moments in classrooms where teacher-pupil roles were reversed or put into a more equitable balance were pivotal in helping them to build real momentum in terms of creative change in classrooms and sometimes across the whole school (this will be explored further in the chapter focusing on 'ethos'). In Creative Partnerships, co-learning appeared to generate a greater sense of 'ease' and well-being amongst pupils; the status of 'learner' being shared by pupils, teachers and artists in the project helped to clearly demarcate the experience as being less about achieving a grade, and more a process of joint discovery. This seemed to be helpful to pupils. Practitioners generally modelled this principle through the kind of discourse they employed, generally using language that was inclusive. It is worthwhile encouraging artists (where it is needed; it often isn't) not to mimic or approximate their own discourse to that of the school. Part of the value they bring is to help everyone involved enjoy learning and to do so using the specific skills, language and ways of thinking that have become habituated through their non-education practice.

Fascination/engagement

In implementing Creative Partnerships, we noted that fascination and engagement was evidenced most often through highly-motivated, happy young people and adults who clearly enjoyed what they were doing. The pleasure of finding things out and making things happen independently, and in ways that were felt to have authenticity, usually led to a sense of engagement and the persistent attention we associate with fascination. It is worth keeping in mind examples of learner motivation that extend beyond the project. Are children following on with work or exploration of new themes outside of the classroom? It is worth considering which projects rated the highest in this area and what it was about the resources, language and other Inputs that may have led to this outcome.

Risk-taking/confidence

We often found risk was expressed through a proliferation of conditional language in the projects we observed across Creative Partnerships. The 'what if…' questions increased in number, and were encouraged by teachers and artists. We were interested in what kinds of projects gave rise to what types of risk-taking (emotional, physical, intellectual etc.), and as we will see from later chapters, this was one of the areas where artists were able to add a lot of value. Their discourse, their uses of space and materials, their way of approaching tasks by trying things out, rather than following set rules, were all-important enablers of risk. In your own work it is worth reflecting on whether patterns emerging that might suggest certain types/forms of educational practice give rise to productive risk-taking.

Refinement/purposeful outcomes

We observed that opportunities to practise and improve, especially during the early stages of the project when the principle of 'freeplay' was invoked (rather than after the project is finished, as is often the case, as a form of reward) was a precursor of the most purposeful outcomes later. We came to the view that in projects that run over a significant duration refinement, discipline and craft were always important features and gave rise to attributes of persistence and resilience in young people.

Reflection – useful thoughts to keep in mind during the reflection phase

- What has changed in terms of the ideas of the school, practitioner and young people? What was the catalyst for this change within the project? How is it repeatable?
- What has changed in terms of the language used in the school, and by the practitioner and young people? What was the catalyst for this change within the project? How is it repeatable?
- What has changed in terms of the environment of the school? What was the catalyst for this change within the project? How is it repeatable?
- What has changed in terms of the resources of the school? What was the catalyst for this change within the project? How is it repeatable?
- What has changed in terms of the qualities and values of the school, practitioner and young people? What was the catalyst for this change within the project? How is it repeatable?

What you will achieve by asking these questions

Raising these questions will lead to a more focused reflection when the project or series of lessons is complete or about to move onto a new phase. It will encourage consideration of all four stages of the creative project and how outcomes developed in relation to inputs. It will offer you an overview of the characteristics of change that may not be directly evident in the detail of evaluation. It will give you some sense of control of process that can at times feel chaotic, and provides the impetus for making sense of what you see.

Looking for answers to these questions offers clues about groups of ideas or actions that together result in change within a particular project. It is through this analysis that one can begin to see emerging patterns and ways of increasing success for learners. Bentley refers to these as 'ladders of generality' (1999, p. 155) and they are the important footholds we look for when gaining mastery or competence in our profession.

Setting out this approach to planning and evaluation outlines how Creative Partnerships attempted to help build a programme across large numbers of schools in ways that could be unique to each classroom but broadly similar in terms of the main facets underpinning that variety. It gives a flavour of the key concepts we were focusing on and the ways we hoped to encourage all participants to have a shared understanding of what they were jointly attempting to achieve. In the chapters that follow, we will see how these concepts translated to work in schools, how that work was interpreted by teams of researchers, which, in time, allowed Creativity Culture and Education and its members to build a rich understanding of the main elements of the programme.

2 School Stories – How Did Creative Partnerships Work in Practice?

Having set out the basic elements of the Creative Partnerships programme, this chapter begins to look at how it worked in practice. Many schools got involved in the programme because of their ambitions to 'change'. Sometimes this was manifest through alterations to the learning environment – for example, the transformation of outdoor spaces – at other times through development of staff or changes to curriculum planning, and sometimes through a blend of all these and more. Using a series of school 'snapshots' from the publication *Changing Young Lives* (BOP Consulting, 2012), this chapter tries to describe what change looked and felt like in schools who implemented the Creative Partnerships programme, and what scale of transformation was possible.[3] Each snapshot will summarise the context each school operated in, their ambitions and goals for their Creative Partnerships work, how each project took shape and the kinds of outcomes it led to.

The Arnold Centre, Rotherham

School background

Arnold Nursery School is a part of The Arnold Centre, which provides education and childcare for children from birth to five years. It gained Early Excellence status in 2002 and was recognised by the Department for Education as a Children's Centre in 2006. It is located in a socially and economically deprived part of Rotherham in South Yorkshire, in the middle of three council estates. The children's standards when they enter the nursery are well below average, particularly in language and communication. Most of the children come from white British backgrounds, with an increasing proportion from Asian backgrounds. A few children are asylum seekers. A high proportion of children have identified learning difficulties or disabilities.

Why did the school first apply to Creative Partnerships?

Prior to involvement with Creative Partnerships for an Enquiry project, the school had occasionally worked with artists on an ad-hoc basis, but (they adopted the Creative Partnerships programme in 2007) this was the first time it had worked with artists to pursue some of the aims of their whole-school plan.

Many pupils enter the nursery with low levels of language and communications skills, and many have little experience of the local community or the wider environment, a lack of richness of experience that hampers the development of communication skills. The school therefore prioritises the development of language, communication and literacy in its School Development Plan and this project was specifically planned to assist this.

One of the main outcomes from the Creative Partnerships Programme that the school wanted to achieve was to **develop language skills through an inspiring exploration of environment and by involving parents:** in this school parents were often little engaged in their children's learning. They wanted to give families experiences that they would not normally have. It was **important to draw in parents** in ways that were non-threatening, and a participative creative project was considered to be perfect for this. The hope was that parents would recognise the **value of supporting their children's learning** and continue to be involved with their children's education and with the nursery after the project finished.

In theory, the Enquiry project chosen would enable children and their parents to create pieces of work together, drawing language out of the children and drawing parents into their children's education and school experiences. Language skills would be developed through planning and discussion and through the shared experience of visits to look at art and sculpture.

The enquiry question chosen by the school to encapsulate this project was: '**What effect does parental involvement have on a child's ability to work creatively, and how does it impact on levels of communication, self-esteem and achievement?**'

What was the project?

The Enquiry project chosen had three phases, all exploring sculpture, environment and art which were all connected through the story of 'Goldilocks and the Three Bears'. The Goldilocks story proved a valuable linking theme, familiar and comfortable to all the families, with opportunities to engage in a language-based discussion about comparative size (small, medium and large). The three phases also enabled the school to target different groups of children and to attract different groups of parents, through their varying emphases, and the skills and qualities of the three artists who led each phase.

First, the school took a group of children and their parents to Yorkshire Sculpture Park to see the work of the artist Sophie Ryder, which involved an exhibition of a number of immense animal sculptures. The families looked at a variety of sculpture and even made their own sculptures while at the park, and once back at school continued the work in the nursery with an artist, using the same kinds of large-scale natural materials as the sculpture park.

The second phase targeted fathers, who are often more difficult to engage than mothers. The school wanted fathers to be casually pulled in by curiosity, and so commissioned a sculptor to produce a large-scale sculpture in wood in the playground. Although the head teacher and creative agent were aware that this was perhaps a stereotyping of gender interests, it was certainly a successful strategy. Fathers who would probably not have actively volunteered to come into school were drawn in by the sight of the chainsaw, the noise and the scale of the project, and the children loved the spectacle and the play potential of the sawdust. This project also enabled the school to make progress on another of its priorities: to integrate indoor and outdoor spaces, providing the same quality of learning environments in each space. The area with the sculpture is now used as a storytelling space and a meeting point, giving the work a lasting legacy.

In the third phase, an artist worked intensively with a group of parents and children. In some ways the work was low key, without large-scale products or outputs, but the quality of work and of discussion was very high. Carrying on the Goldilocks theme, children and parents made small, medium and large books, cushions and hands of friendship.

What were the impacts of the project?

Impact on parents

Each of the three phases attracted parents in different ways chiefly because of the different ways the artists worked and the various opportunities parents were provided with to contribute. Many **parents were profoundly influenced by their involvement**. One parent began to come in regularly to talk to staff, two or three mums set up their own group to do similar work without an artist to support them, which continued until their children moved on to primary school, and a parents' group was set up. The school also planned to consolidate this enthusiasm with a creative day for children and parents and regular Saturday activities. In the longer term, the school aspired to have a permanent 'atelier' resource: materials permanently on hand for making sculptural work such as wood, rope, cogs, clay, and so on. The creative agent described all of these as 'little nuggets of starting points'. For her, 'Enquiry projects are all about this: not incredible resolutions, but starting the questioning.'

It is worth emphasising the different roles adopted by creative agents in the programme as opposed to artists. Creative agents were overseers of projects in schools and acted as brokers and interpreters between educators and artists, ensuring the needs of the school were met by the specific skills and attributes of particular artists. Creative agents would also work with senior staff in schools to help embed learning across the curriculum and build future projects into long-term planning cycles. The artists themselves were focused on specific project outcomes and were expected to bring their artform specialisms to bear on defined questions and challenges the school had previously identified with the help of the creative agent.

The nursery head teacher, Margaret Hague, felt that **creative work was particularly good to engage parents**, simply because it was unthreatening, enjoyable, relaxing: it made parents want to have a go themselves, and unlike maths or science, no one could feel there were right and wrong ways to do it.

Impact on young people

Most of the children at The Arnold Centre not only arrive with poor language, but often with a paucity of experience on which to use their language skills. One of the key impacts of the project was that at **all stages produced more sophisticated language from the children**, such as developing an ability to use mathematical terms related to size and scale, and to discuss their work using creative technical terms. Teachers observed that children had real understanding of the concepts they were using. However, perhaps **the most valuable language improvement was in communication between children and their parents.** Families had to negotiate exactly how projects would be undertaken, who would do what and how to resolve problems that arose. The feeling of the school was that this was a much richer exchange than these families might usually engage in.

Impact on the school

The school had extensive plans to build on the gains made here: as previously mentioned, the parents set up a Saturday activity group, and they collected sculptural materials so that more sculpture could be made by children and their families. Overall, the approach **proved a very successful way of bringing parents into the**

life of the school. Staff also learnt to use wider approaches and different creative techniques from each of the three artists involved.

Impact on creative providers

The four artists involved in this project varied in their experience of working in these contexts. For instance, the creative agent, who had worked with Creative Partnerships for several years, felt that her learning curve on this project was not steep, while one of the artists involved had to change their initially over-ambitious plans and re-gauge the work to fit the circumstances.

What made the project successful?

After an initial meticulous planning process the creative agent handed most of the responsibility for the project to the school itself. She felt it was important that they were in charge of what happened and she also thought that schools had become more demanding over the years in what they wanted from working with creative practitioners. This confidence and equal partnership is an important factor in the success of all Creative Partnership projects.

The variety of approaches and media chosen by different artists in each of the three phases also enabled everybody to get something out of some part of the work, but the strong connecting threads of the environmental theme and the Goldilocks story gave the project an overarching and simple cohesion.

What followed the project at this school?

The project was highly successful in bringing parents into a partnership with their children's school, and led to exciting plans to harness this new enthusiasm and build on the relationships. Perhaps what was most encouraging about these plans was that they originated not with the school itself, but with the parents' own enthusiasm and desire to continue engagement.

Three years later

Activities at The Arnold Centre

Since taking part in the Creative Partnerships project described above, The Arnold Centre has increasingly integrated creativity into their school. This was done by focusing on the development of what head teacher Margaret Hague called a 'more holistic creative approach' within the whole school's curriculum, based on supporting children's creative development.

Whilst The Arnold Centre did not engage in new projects supported by Creative Partnerships, they have continued to use the ideas and skills gained during the initial project and have run many similar projects since then. As in their original project, these have focused on integrating the pupils' parents, and have included activities both in the school's inside and outside areas.

As the large-scale model work created with the creative practitioners during the Enquiry project was so successful, this has been repeated several times, resulting in the building of large objects such as a spaceship, a dragon and similar objects which now decorate the school grounds as 'outside land art'. These were created during regular Saturday and holiday group activities, which heavily involve the pupils' parents, who often bring their own ideas. By using scrap metal and collected junk for the sculptures, the school can ensure it uses the funds available for such projects carefully, with the aim of running as many projects as possible. The school has also introduced 'Stay, Play and Make-days', which take place at least once every half term. They are based on a variety of themes, again involve the parents who come in to take part in creative activities with their children. As planned, workshop areas have been established in all the nursery rooms, which the children are able to use independently and which are used for joint activities with the parents. The school has invested in a moveable unit that can be pushed between classrooms, carrying a variety of craft materials for the pupils to create collages, pictures, picture frames and more.

Long-term impact of the project

As head teacher Margaret Hague noted, the expertise of the Creative Partnership practitioners who supported the initial projects clearly sparked an interest within the school staff; with three different artists involved in the projects each giving staff different inspirations and ideas. Through providing a choice of different artistic forms, everyone could identify with a project. Teachers have since then become visibly more confident in using the experiences gained, transferring them to other curriculum areas and trying out new creative activities. They have also been able to pass their new knowledge on to other staff at the Centre.

In this way, the idea of a more creative approach to teaching has permeated through the entire staff at The Arnold Centre, making it an institution-wide approach to teaching. As a nursery school within a children's centre, other areas of the centre are also included in this. The centre's community outreach worker now arranges weekly events for parents and children and offers creative weekend and holiday activities. This ensures that the centre is open with creative activities readily accessible to pupils and parents all year round.

Staff are also continuing to look into new ways of bringing creative and cross-cutting approaches to the curriculum. For example, they use a wide range of creative activities on a large and small scale, particularly drawing and painting, to develop children's fine and gross motor skills. From this strong base children quickly learn their first writing skills which form the foundation for learning to write in the future.

A further important aim that The Arnold Centre is focusing on through their creative activities is the development of their pupils' independence. For example, children have independent access to the nursery room workshop areas and are given the choice of which materials they would like to work with, thus encouraging and developing their ability to make decisions for themselves. As a nursery school, children only stay at The Arnold Centre for one year, before going on to primary school. Whilst this leaves little room to assess the long-term impact these activities have on the pupils, the above examples show that activities are clearly geared towards this situation. As Margaret Hague explained, the overall teaching focus is not only based on knowledge, but also on providing children with new transferrable skills which will form a valuable basis for their learning in the future.

As the initial project focused on improving parents' involvement in their children's school activities, this aspect has continued to play an important part in all The Arnold Centre's creative work. Margaret Hague again stressed the importance of creative activities in encouraging parents to be more involved in their children's school life. As she commented, the families do not feel threatened by the idea of 'making things' in a way they might if they were asked to take part in 'numeracy skills' activities or similar, and are thus much more likely to participate in creative activities. The school continues to run their Saturday morning 'dads' groups', which are regularly attended by around ten fathers. Here, participants are encouraged to engage in more 'tactile, messy' work with their children – one recent example included 'den-building'. Parents enthusiastically bring in their own ideas and skills, are becoming more confident and are taking an active part in ensuring the continuation of these events.

Crucially, it seems that once parents engage in these activities with their children within the school environment, they are much more likely to take these new skills and ideas home with them and use them in the family environment. As the head teacher observed, this continues to be the case and children regularly tell their teachers about the activities they engage in with their parents at home. This is also transferred to the pupils' siblings, who are often brought along to participate in the activities at the school. This means that, in effect, children often benefit from The Arnold Centre's activities for longer than they are actually pupils there. Another more indirect impact on the parents is that through taking part in the activities at

The Arnold Centre, they are becoming more used to the school environment and have less reservation about engaging with schools and teachers. As a result, parents are also more likely to take an active interest in their children's school life once they have moved on to primary school.

Future plans

The Arnold Centre's creative activities are set to continue in the future and are clearly very much supported by the head teacher, who stressed the importance of providing children with 'creative ways to get them involved in the environment and in learning'. Whilst staff have already become visibly more skilled in developing creative ideas, the school is nevertheless keen to continue developing their skills and is looking at different ways of including the arts and creativity in the curriculum. As part of this, there are plans for further relevant training days in the next year for both staff and parents, seeking to provide as many people as possible with the insights and experiences in creative teaching which have already been gained. Furthermore, The Arnold Centre welcomes the opportunity to share ideas with other local infant and nursery schools, some of which took part in Creative Partnerships projects themselves. They are thus part of a 'learning community' in which new ideas and activities are exchanged and schools benefit from each others' experiences. The Arnold Centre also frequently receives visitors from early years practitioners or neighbouring Local Authorities who are keen to learn about the approaches taken at the school in particular in respect to their creative activities. It seems that The Arnold Centre has developed a reputation for creative teaching within the teaching community – not least supported by the fact that they were awarded the Quality Mark by the Alliance for Lifelong Learning, an acknowledgement of good practice in literacy, language and numeracy for children and young people.

Future creative activities are already being planned, such as a Christmas event, which will include performances of traditional stories and the building of a 'garden room' to provide children with an outside creative learning space. Whilst the school has not yet explored possible alternative sources of funding, this is something they are planning to do in the future, seeking to supplement a school budget that has already become noticeably tighter. Nevertheless, Margaret Hague stressed that The Arnold Centre has well adapted to stretch their funds as far as possible. Moreover, the school has a good adult-child ratio based on the keen enthusiasm shown by both teachers and parents, who often volunteer to participate in the activities. This, in the end, is the best proof of the success of The Arnold Centre's activities – and provides confidence that they will be able to continue with their activities in the future.

Lancasterian Special School, West Didsbury

School background

Lancasterian School is a special school that caters for pupils with a wide range of physical disabilities and severe medical conditions. Many of the pupils have complex needs including learning and communication difficulties. The school offers provision for children and young people up to 16 years old through foundation, into primary and up to secondary school.

They pride themselves on offering comprehensive speech and language therapy, occupational therapy, physical therapy and medical support within the school alongside the normal school life. The team of dedicated staff have a range of expertise and are committed to support the learning needs of the pupils. Lancasterian believes every pupil has the right to a voice to express their opinions and views.

The pupils follow the national curriculum at their own specific level. Their learning and access to the curriculum is enhanced by specialist resources. These include sophisticated communication aids and other equipment which support the pupils' physical access needs. They also aim to provide opportunities for pupils to learn about and begin to understand the diversity of beliefs and cultures, including minority cultures present in modern Britain. The school encourages pupils to acquire independence, self-control and to take responsibility for their learning and development.

Although the school had no prior involvement with Creative Partnerships before it engaged in its project it has had an ongoing commitment to creativity and creative learning for many years.

Why did the school apply to Creative Partnerships?

In 2007, the school had just developed an 'environment control room'; this was a space that contained a range of programmable lights, sounds and effects. The idea was for this to be a fully accessible environment where pupils could engage in the curriculum. However, although the room had a lot of potential, neither staff nor pupils had experienced its full capabilities so far.

The assistant head teacher was given the remit to **improve creativity within the school** as well as oversee the School Development Plan. One of the main priorities of this School Development Plan was to **raise the quality of teaching and learning through the continued development of personalised provision** with the help of the new environmental control room. As such, the school felt that the opportunity to apply for an Enquiry School project came along at an ideal time.

The school asked the following enquiry question to encapsulate their project: **'Using the multimedia room (environment room) and its equipment, can we develop the creative skills of our pupils, who have very limited experience of the outside world as a result of reduced mobility and medical conditions?'**

Sadly, many of the pupils' imaginations are profoundly underdeveloped as result of their physical and medical conditions. In answering this question, Lancasterian wanted to be able to **develop the pupils' interest in the world by encouraging them to become more creative in their ideas, and in turn more enthusiastic about their learning experience**.

What was the project?

The creative agent working on this project facilitated and then brokered a partnership between the Workers Film Association (WFA) and Lancasterian School. At this point, the WFA had three years experience of working with special needs schools. As an organisation it has a wealth of experience and excellent new media tools and techniques. These are ideally suited to giving young people a voice and helping them share their ideas, experiences and aspirations with a wider audience through the dynamic and creative process of film-making. The WFA approach fitted well within the school and its school improvement plan.

This Enquiry School Project was split into two phases:

1 In the first phase the pupils created characters together and then drew them on simple (computer) Paint programs. These were then dropped into a PowerPoint file where other students created backgrounds and storyboarded ideas. All the students added sound and animation effects to the overall presentation.

2 The second phase involved the older students mentoring the new students in the techniques they had previously learnt. Students decided on new characters and storylines, this time choosing to enact the parts. The students designed and made all the costumes, as well as scripting and acting the parts. Finally, the students edited film themselves.

What were the impacts of the project?

Impact on young people

Lancasterian made good progress in **developing the pupils' creative skills**. These would eventually impact on the pupils' learning experiences and their perception of the world.

The co-ordinating teacher working on this project commented that it had allowed them to discover hidden talents in the pupils. One pupil, for example, who had never used the particular Paint program before, in fact the staff had not even known that he was artistic, took to it very quickly and concentrated for long periods of time. School staff encouraged him to develop his interest, which led him to take a course in computer graphics. Another pupil was offered work experience by the WFA as a result of his involvement in this Enquiry project.

The pupils really listened to the artists and were inspired by each other's work and ideas. The use of multimedia added another dimension to the pupils' creativity and learning styles. Many of the pupils have memory recall issues and would not normally have had such clear recollection of events. But as a result of the project, several pupils asked to have the programs they used in the sessions put on their laptops so they could use them at home: this indicated the **development of ideas and retention of skills**. Furthermore, pupils really engaged in the sessions and often asked members of staff when the artists were coming in next. There was also considerable impact upon the **confidence and communication skills** of pupils. Some more reticent or shy pupils became increasingly forthcoming and eager to be involved in the project as it progressed. For example, an autistic student who rarely initiated conversation began making suggestions.

Whenever the project was running, there was an unexpected energy and buzz that ran through the senior school. Pupils were **talking more, asking** and **answering more questions, listening** and then **reflecting. Peer mentoring** had also been an unexpected outcome from the project, with pupils fully embraced the 'mentoring' role.

Impact on the school

The project allowed Lancasterian staff to realise that they needed to broaden their horizons. The teachers learnt to **allow pupils to use their own initiative**. In a special needs context, it is common for staff to become controlling over the structure of the lesson, normally planning every minute, thus possibly missing other outcomes by being too inflexible.

Due to the success of the project, it was also decided that WFA should run a subsequent Continuing Profession Development (CPD) session for the school staff at Lancasterian, to allow staff to develop a clear perception of what is possible through digital media.

Impacts on creative partner

Although they had previously worked with some special needs schools in the past, the WFA had not worked with pupils that have the specific types of communication requirements of Lancasterian pupils, and this project therefore represented a valuable working experience for them. To maximise the experience, WFA staff involved in the project were asked to **pass on the learning from their work with the Lancasterian pupils to the team of artists** WFA works with, who come from different art disciplines and work with a wide range of groups and organisations.

What made the project so successful?

The project was highly successful in providing the Lancasterian pupils with a voice. The role of the creative agent, Jude Bird, was a key factor in the success of the project. She provided invaluable advice in both the application and planning phases. 'As a school, we can't thank her enough for brokering the partnership with WFA. They are a fantastic contact, who have considerable experience and expertise at working with children with special needs.'

What followed the project?

Following the above project, the school applied for **specialist status in communication and interaction**, seeking to access additional funding which would allow them to further develop services for their pupils. The application did indeed prove successful and the co-ordinating teacher felt at the time that the school's involvement in the Enquiry School project helped them gain the specialist status. The application was made in order to have a huge impact on the pupils learning, their quality of life and their ability to lead exciting and fulfilling lives. The school wanted to empower their pupils, to give them the one thing they could control: finding their voices and leading the lives they deserve. Amongst other things, the additional funds were thus used for substantial building alterations to provide pupils with a 'skills base and social area' within the school, and to employ a speech and language therapist.

The creative partner involved, WFA also asked the school to get involved in another project outside of Creative Partnerships. This next project, focusing on the creation and use of puppets, aimed to allow pupils in Key Stage 3 to benefit from some of the outcomes the other pupils had gained during the Enquiry School project.

Most directly, the school continued to use their ICT equipment in lessons as introduced during the Creative Partnerships project, and pupils remain busy creating new storyboards or using techniques such as stop-start animation to create short films. Staff took the skills they gained during the project and, supported by a range of CPD events delivered by both the practitioners and by teachers who took part in the projects, were able to transfer these skills to new subjects and ideas. For example, ICT was used for a series of lessons discussing fairy tales with younger pupils.

Three years later

Lancasterian School's Change School Programme

In September 2010, Lancasterian School became a Creative Partnerships Change School after being approached by their former creative agent, Jude Bird. Jude had initially been working with a different school, but when this fell through suggested that Lancasterian School take over the previous school's Change School status. The idea was to create a new three-year Change School project to be run within the one remaining funded year of the Change School programme. Lancasterian were happy to accept, and with Jude's help created their own Change School programme.

The programme included three separate strands: the development of the school's outdoor area with the help of an expert practitioner, projects on the theme of 'finding our voices' working with different year groups, and a targeted workforce development project. As part of the 'finding our voices' project, pupils in Key Stage 3 worked with a disabled theatre group, resulting in a joint staged performance. At the same time, Key Stage 4 pupils worked with a poet, writing their own poetry, which was subsequently presented at a Specialist Schools Conference. Each of the pupils involved received a copy, and the school has successfully sold the book at various events and conferences they have taken part in. For both groups, the project represented an important way to develop pupils' creative and communicative skills.

The workforce development project specifically addressed the relationship between the school's teaching staff and physiotherapy staff in Key Stage 1, which has been greatly enhanced since the project. Both sets of staff received relevant training together, delivered by creative practitioners, in this case dance professionals, to bring therapy and dance elements into the classroom. This joint approach, in which the teaching and physiotherapy staff's skills complemented each other during the training, has proven so successful that further CPD events like this have taken place. The school is now planning for teachers across the school to take part, with the aim of bringing the benefits to other older year groups as well.

The school also regularly runs 'Creative Thursdays' – afternoon classes for primary and foundation years which include pupils from local mainstream schools. Together, the children work on creative activities which don't fit into normal lessons, such as photography, artwork, gardening or eco-themes. Although these events were already running before the school's initial Creative Partnerships project, many of the ideas gained during Creative Partnerships activities have filtered into these sessions.

Long-term impact of the project

Four years on, many of the approaches and techniques introduced during the initial ICT project and subsequent Creative Partnerships activities continue to be used in different subject areas throughout the school.

Impact on young people

As seen above, Lancasterian has a strong focus on supporting pupils' communication skills. For example, this is reflected in the school's decision to use part of their specialist status grant to pay for a speech and language therapist who has worked intensively with the pupils. Many of the creative activities also feed into this objective: peer-to-peer mentoring and the idea of 'buddying-up' younger and more advanced pupils, which has become a regular feature of school life. Pupils thus support each other in their maths tasks, shared reading exercises or in creative activities such as devising their own games. This approach has been successfully introduced even to the school's primary department. Pupils find it extremely useful and by explaining what they have learnt themselves to younger pupils they deepen their own knowledge, whilst at the same time gaining new communication skills and increased confidence in themselves.

A further substantial impact was gained through Creative Partnerships' focus on bringing in expert practitioners to work with the pupils. This worked so well that since the initial project, Lancasterian School has brought in many other experts to work with the children on a variety of projects or subjects, including dance, poetry or theatre activities. The assistant head teacher, Kira Buhler, explained that this approach is so successful because 'outsiders' brought into the school often have new and different ways of looking at and reacting to the pupils. Children consequently often react differently to these 'outsiders' than to their regular teachers; they appear inspired by the new faces and ideas and enthusiastically rise to the tasks they have been given.

Impact on the school

Head teacher Kira Buhler feels that the projects had the most far-reaching impact in terms of the new practices and procedures they introduced to staff.

For example, another important part of the initial project that has been extremely useful to the school was the new project recording and observation approach it introduced to the school. Baseline techniques were used to assess how the children developed and responded over several weeks. This gave teachers new tools to better assess pupils' development throughout both the initial and all subsequent projects, and in turn means that staff are better able to fine-tune projects for maximum impact.

Furthermore, the teachers themselves have also substantially gained from the creative practitioners brought in for the projects. Teachers were able to observe the activities led by the practitioners, and in many cases could adopt – and adapt – new ideas for their own lessons.

Future plans

Kira Buhler stressed that creativity will continue to remain high on the school's agenda in the future. As part of the senior management team at the school, she herself is responsible for bringing creativity into the school life, making sure that the school is open to exciting and innovative ways of teaching. To firmly embed creativity within the entire school, Lancasterian School has in the past years continued to heavily invest in their staff, both through internal CPD events and through bringing in outside support. They have also included 'creativity' within their School Development Plan and have written a creative curriculum for the school. This seeks to embed creativity in all lessons taught at the school, bearing in mind the questions such as: What do we want to deliver to the children? What do they need? How can we teach them in ways that are appropriate to them? As part of this, the school is particularly keen to further develop their cross-curricular activities, avoiding subjects being delivered in isolation. For example, Key Stage 3 pupils recently completed an enterprise project in which they created their own music DVD, drawing on a variety of different subjects in the process.

Whilst being aware that it will be difficult in future to find large sums of funding for creative projects, Kira Buhler seemed confident that Lancasterian School would be able to find some alternative, smaller sources of funding for new projects.

The school plan to continue inviting practitioners to run short creative projects in the future. However, they also feel they have learnt many things that could be repeated in a 'smaller way' in the future. For example, expert practitioners could continue to be invited into the school but for shorter periods of time, to keep costs down. Importantly, the school has also developed links with other Creative Partnerships special educational needs schools which they met through their Creative Partnerships activities, and are actively engaged in exchanging ideas with these schools through peer-to-peer mentoring between school staff. Similarly, the school has established links with five other schools (primary and secondary), as well as community partners such as the local police force, who they have supported with the help of their speech and language therapist and the expertise the school has built up in this area. Lancasterian School clearly feels that it will continue to benefit from exchanging experiences between the school's staff and a variety of external partners – something that can be attained on a reciprocal basis, without the need for large sums of funding.

Minterne Community Junior School, Sittingbourne

School background

Minterne Junior School in Sittingbourne, Kent, is a large community primary school with around 400 pupils. The school has an attached unit for pupils with speech and language difficulties, and a higher than average proportion of pupils with special educational needs. It has a below-average proportion of pupils from minority ethnic backgrounds and a low proportion of pupils eligible for free school meals.

Why did the school join the Creative Partnerships programme?

Minterne Junior School first became involved with Creative Partnerships in early 2006. In the previous year, the school had been graded 'satisfactory' in their Ofsted report. The head teacher, Bill McGrory, said that whilst pupils were well behaved, they seemed passive. They were not as engaged or enthused by the lessons as they could have been. The lessons were well planned, but subjects were taught separately in subject boxes, more along the lines of a secondary school.

Looking for ways to turn this situation around, the head and deputy head teacher went on a one-day course on 'Re-exciting/Re-igniting the Primary Curriculum' run by HMI inspectors. They came back planning to 'do things differently' and **to start**

teaching in a more creative way by developing a more engaging curriculum. They met with resistance from staff to begin with. Bill McGrory noted that they were reluctant to leave the 'comfort zones' of their established plans. Nevertheless, the head and deputy head decided to forge ahead, trialling the new approach in Year 5.

Within three months of trialling the new curriculum, Minterne was approached by Creative Partnerships, who invited the school to work with them. Becoming a Creative Partnerships School seemed like the obvious next step and Minterne accepted. As a result, Minterne was able to **involve all year groups in creative activities**.

What was the project?

Minterne's first Creative Partnerships project, 'Re-exciting/Re-igniting', began in 2006. Each year group looked at one subject area that teachers felt had become 'stale'. A creative practitioner met with each year group in turn to exchange ideas on how this area could be made more creative. This artist was particularly good at supporting staff in **'thinking outside the box'**, and had the skills needed to translate plans into realities. The emphasis in that first year was on transforming space in the classroom. With three teachers in each year group, all of Minterne's teachers were involved in the Creative Partnerships projects right from the beginning.

Year 4 focused on astronomy and did a 'sky and space' project in which children created planets out of papier-mâché, re-creating the solar system in the classroom. Year 5 looked at new ways of teaching religious education and decided to run a project on Buddhism. With the help of the artist, the teachers transformed a classroom into a Buddhist temple, and all staff and children wore Buddhist robes throughout the week. All learning and teaching took place in this space with not a textbook or desk in sight. On the last day, a Buddhist monk from Canterbury visited the 'Minterne temple' to lead a meditation session. Year 6 're-excited' a local history project on neighbouring Borden village. Together with the artist, children took photographs of the buildings and constructed a detailed replica of Borden made of cardboard boxes. This was displayed in the school hall, enabling the children to learn about the village in a much more hands-on and engaging way.

What were the project impacts?

According to the head teacher, all these projects were a resounding success, liberating the teachers from their set ways of working. The Buddhist project in particular was so successful that it has become an established part of the school's curriculum.

Impact on young people

The projects seemed to have an immediate and visible effect on the children involved. They were much **more engaged in their work** than before, with the Year 6 pupils who recreated Borden village being eager to take responsibility for the project. Crucially, by **experiencing a subject, rather than just hearing** about it, pupils seemed to find it much easier to remember what they had learnt. The teachers were delighted with the outcome. The same outcome was seen in children in Year 4. When building the solar system, they talked about the individual planets they were constructing. At the end of the project, pupils had visibly taken information on board much better than usual – when asked questions, they were all eager to demonstrate that they knew what Saturn looked like, or where in the solar system they would find Pluto.

Impact on the teachers

Whilst staff at Minterne were initially wary of adopting new ways of teaching, this changed rapidly when the creative practitioners came on board. The teachers gained as much as the children from the new ideas and expertise. They became quickly aware of the visible impact that the projects were having on pupil engagement and were soon convinced by this more creative approach to teaching. Bill McGrory recalls how one teacher working on the planet project told him she felt they were 'wasting time' building the planets which could have been spent teaching pupils about them instead. Weeks later, the teacher returned to Bill to tell him how much better the children seemed to have taken the information on board. Looking back, Bill commented that despite the initial resistance, all teachers were fully convinced by this more creative way of teaching within the first year.

What made the project successful?

The year group projects were successful because they created 'memorable experiences'. The children were able to engage in, relate to and remember these experiences for a long time. Crucially, along with the memory of the event, the learning itself had also been more firmly embedded.

Bill emphasised that the school never lost sight of its overall aim of improving standards. The school had clear learning aims that the creative projects complemented. The creative practitioner who was brought in to support the projects was clearly aware of this and worked together with the teachers very effectively.

Three years later

Minterne: A Creative Partnerships Enquiry School

Since this initial project phase, Minterne Junior School has gone from strength to strength, running a number of projects which have grown in ambition and scale along the way.

In late 2007, Minterne became a Creative Partnerships Enquiry School. In the autumn of that year, the Chinese Terracotta army was exhibited at the British Museum and this inspired the teachers to create a 'China Week' at the school. All pupils visited the museum, and back at school children created their own Terracotta Army of 400 clay figures, which proudly guarded a model of the school building. Parents were invited to see Minterne's exhibition which was, in the head teacher's words, an 'amazing sight'. At this point, it was felt the school had 'cracked it'. By embracing this project independently, the teachers had shown how much more liberated and confident they felt to take risks in order to involve pupils in engaging projects. In the same year, working as an Enquiry School, Minterne also celebrated 'Monster Week', a week of activities based on the old English legend of Beowulf and Grendel. These projects focused on writing and raising pupils' writing standards. This was a whole-school issue, identified in the School Improvement Plan. Children created their own Grendel monsters and in an end of project event, shared what they had written, drawn and created at an exhibition to which parents and grandparents were again invited. As both these project weeks show, Minterne tries to build in a home link into all their activities, engaging parents and inviting them to the school.

Minterne's Change School Programme

Following the Enquiry School project, Minterne Junior School successfully applied to join the Creative Partnerships Change School programme, which they took part in from 2008/09 to 2010/11.

In their first year as a Change School, and third year with Creative Partnerships, Minterne decided to focus on a 'Green' theme that would involve pupil voice as much as possible. The idea was that pupils themselves would be the driving force of the project. To this end, the School Council and Green Team worked alongside teachers, governors and the creative practitioner to develop the programme. This included creating topical films and organising an event, attended by the mayor and the pupils' parents. In 2009, the whole school was again involved in various projects. In Year 5, as part of their Tudor topic, they recreated the 'Field of Cloth of Gold'. The project culminated in a Tudor festival during which the children were dressed up in Tudor costumes, learnt Tudor dances, took part in storytelling events and even engaged in (risk-free) 'jousting' tournaments. Parents were invited to the festivities and, as Bill McGrory said, the whole event was a truly memorable experience for the children. The Year 3 project that year was entitled 'Memories'. Children recreated their memories through song, dance, drama, art and poetry. Considering the age of the children, the work was remarkably mature, insightful and poignant.

As with all previous projects, the emphasis was on quality experiences with quality outcomes and a direct link to the School Improvement Plan. Although children were clearly enthused by the activities, the objective was never simply to have fun. **Raising standards through a creative and engaging curriculum was always the main priority**. This, as Bill McGrory explains, is where the link between teachers and artists, and their ability to work closely together, is particularly important. Over the years, Minterne has learnt **that it is essential to ensure that there are quality learning outcomes** from the school's engagement with the creative practitioners. Working with artists' needs brings added value to what the children learn. The teachers can focus on the curriculum needs and how to put these across, and this work can be enhanced through the skills of the practitioner. Moreover, the school feels it is fundamentally important that the children's exercise books reflect the quality of the experiences. Through lessons learnt in earlier projects, the school had also realised the importance of providing staff with sufficient time for planning. Quality time is needed for staff to combine the creative elements with the requirements of the curriculum. Thus for the above projects teachers were able to go off site in year groups for a day of preparation.

Even with this knowledge and experience, there is no guarantee of success. In 2009/10 Minterne's project was entitled 'Boys' Zone'. The practitioners provided 'boy-friendly' activities and collected data in a study examining boys' learning. Although the children enjoyed the activities, the resulting research lacked academic rigour. In retrospect, the school felt that requiring artists to act as researchers is not playing to their strengths, as research tasks need to be carried out by experienced researchers. This was a learning experience for both the school and the artists. Nevertheless, the school's confidence in the artists was not diminished by this experience and they were subsequently involved in successful projects the following year.

More recently, the school has been engaged in a project on the subject of 'flow', a concept which analyses people's engagement with an activity and which was described by the psychologist Mihaly Csikszentmihalyi in his book of the same name (1991). The level of challenge in the activity needs to match the level of skill and when people are in 'flow', time passes quickly. Flow is linked to human happiness and whilst the experience of it varies between children, it can occur in any subject from arts to maths and science. The school was keen to identify where this occurred in school and to maximise its potential. The project was led by Jonathan Barnes, a practitioner from Canterbury Christ Church University and an expert on the subject of creativity and engagement. He introduced staff to the concept of 'flow' as well as to ways of assessing it. Teachers then looked at 'flow' together with the children, sharing and discussing ideas. The pupils were asked to think about where they experienced 'flow', both in school and at home, with the aim of helping them identify this concept themselves. As part of the project, the school ran a 'Flow Day' with workshops, questionnaires and a variety of activities including cooking, dancing, maths and drama, aimed at seeing 'what makes the children tick, what makes them happy'. This provided the school with valuable insight into how teachers can provide more flow-inducing elements to their lessons in the future.

Long-term impact

In line with the school's focus on outcome-based projects which tie in with the School Improvement Plan, there has been a clear development in the aims the school has been pursuing with its creative projects over the years. Whilst the first year aimed at getting staff to 'think outside the box' and take some risks in terms of lesson delivery, the second year focused on the pupils' writing skills – an issue that had been picked up in the 2008 Ofsted report. In recent years, Minterne has focused on giving pupils a bigger voice, including them in the discussion and development of new projects.

Minterne's continued progress in developing and delivering creative education has transformed the school into a vibrant place. The head teacher is delighted with the direction the school has taken in recent years and this is fully supported by staff, governors and parents. Importantly, Minterne decided to move away from the subject-based curriculum, which had contributed to passive learning behaviour of the pupils. The curriculum has now been completely re-developed into a cross-curricular teaching approach within each year group, into which creative (cross-curricular) projects can be embedded much more effectively.

Clearly, the school's now long-standing creative approach to teaching has had a substantial impact, not only on its immediate community as a whole, but individually on all those involved. Staff, says Bill McGrory, feeling much more liberated than before are now accustomed to 'thinking outside the box' and are more confident in developing their own creative ideas. Frequently, teachers and practitioners act as co-learners and creative practitioners have also gained useful experiences from working with young children over the years. The teachers have learnt to build on the creative elements brought in by the practitioners and this has brought out their own natural creativity. Moreover, the continued engagement with creative practices led teachers to design the school's Creative Curriculum in late 2009. Whilst initially there was a sharp learning curve and an increase in their workload, teachers could readily see the benefits and so were willing to put in the extra time to reshape the whole school curriculum.

The children themselves are unrecognisable from the passive learners of five years ago. Pupils love developing, creating and engaging in the projects, and this has had a significant impact on their overall enthusiasm and attentiveness during lessons. Some pupils, who have moved on to secondary school, have said that they wished that there could be a 'Minterne Secondary School', evidence of how much they enjoyed their time at their junior school. As a more direct result, the school has also seen the pupils' SAT results improve. In 2010, pupils achieved the best SAT results ever across all subjects, and particularly in writing. This provided clear evidence for the school staff of a link between creativity, pupil engagement and improved test results.

Parents have also felt the impact of the school's creative approach to teaching. They have reported that their children are now far more willing to talk about what they are doing in school. Parents are more frequent visitors to classrooms to see the work at the end of projects. They clearly enjoy coming in to see what their children have been doing at school and consequently seem more involved in their children's school life in general. Children love to share their work with their parents and are keen to show their improving standards.

All these developments and changes are reflected in the school's Ofsted reports. In 2008, Ofsted rated Minterne as 'Good' with an 'Outstanding' curriculum; a clear development from their 2005 'Satisfactory' inspection. The report in particular mentioned the 'memorable experiences' Minterne created through events such as China Week or Monster Week, and picked up on the children's enthusiasm and low levels of absenteeism. Following this, the most recent Ofsted report rated Minterne a straight 'Outstanding' with an 'Outstanding' curriculum. In 2009, the school also applied for the Arts Council's Artsmark for quality arts education and received the Gold Award, another important recognition of the school's achievements.

Minterne's success has not gone unnoticed in the local community and the wider primary education sector. There is now an annual waiting list for the school and other schools are keen to visit. Senior management also frequently give talks about their activities to other schools and groups of head teachers. Other schools are particularly interested in learning more about Minterne's new creative curriculum and the impact it has had on the school.

Future plans

Clearly, creative teaching and learning has come to Minterne to stay. With such a significant impact on staff and pupils, as Bill McGrory says, 'creativity is now part of the school culture – there is no turning back.' This is evidenced by the many plans that the school already has for the future. Additionally, senior management has secured a service level agreement with Future Creative (the independent organisation responsible for Creative Partnerships in Kent), providing Minterne with significant finance to enable it to further work with creative practitioners.

Minterne is also engaged in taking their ideas into the local community and plan to work alongside other schools in Sittingbourne in the future, delivering staff development days and getting pupils to work together. Importantly, their aim is not just to tell other schools about their projects, but to work together, combining experiences and ideas to create joint creative activities. As Bill McGory puts it, in the end, 'it is not so much about funding; it's an attitude.' Even if a lack of funding means Minterne cannot bring in creative practitioners in the future, he is certain that this will not stop them from engaging in similar projects, based on the substantial experience they have gained by now. With this in mind, it looks as if Minterne is set to continue giving children these memorable experiences, which they will be able to talk, write and remember about for a long time to come.

These snapshots of some of the schools that participated in Creative Partnerships are designed to give a flavour of the kinds of projects that took place and the way different sorts of legacy are established in each school. They also hint at some of the challenges around continuity and how fragile positive educational experiences can be for young people if, at moment of school transfer, there is a big shift to a culture that does not place a premium on creative ways of learning.

In the chapters that follow we will consider some of the key themes that emerged from the Creative Partnerships programme in greater depth. By doing so, we will delineate the major features to consider when attempting to build a creative school. We will start by looking first at the concept of school ethos.

3 Creative School Ethos

In schools that developed Creative Partnerships approaches to teaching and learning, we found anecdotal evidence of shifts in ethos. Teachers would talk of a general change in the school, that 'ways of doing things' had changed and developed. From another perspective, it may be that some schools with particular sorts of ethos were attracted to the Creative Partnerships programme. In both cases it seemed to us there was something interesting about 'types' of ethos that seemed to predominate in the programme. In this chapter, I will set out these different types of ethos that developed in some of the schools most deeply engaged in the Creative Partnerships programme, with examples. A shared facet seemed to be an apparent commitment to student voice and putting young people in control of decisions about their own learning. By setting out these particular attributes I hope it will be possible for readers to situate their own schools somewhere within the different kinds of ethos described.

Background – why is ethos important?

Before we begin to consider how Creative Partnerships affected school ethos I want to first set out a broader context for the debate about school ethos as a whole. In what ways has ethos become a significant educational concept now? In their research for CCE, Bragg and Manchester (2011) set out a number of likely reasons why ethos has gained currency within the educational arena.

The first reason is to do with variation in schools as the education sector becomes more influenced by market forces. Bragg and Manchester point out that since the 1988 Education Act, the school system in England and Wales has passed through various reforms, all of which had the effect of encouraging greater diversity of educational provision (pp. 9–10). A direct consequence of this has been a greater perceived need to 'sell' the distinctive virtues of a particular school in relation to those of a near neighbour. Bragg and Manchester go on to show how decades of government policies have explicitly encouraged this process of marketisation (pp. 9–10). Ethos, in such a context, becomes an aspect of marketing a school to parents and the wider community.

The other key reason for the current interest in school ethos is the kind of power and influence ethos is felt to exert over learners – as Bragg and Manchester put it, an interest 'in what it "does" rather than what it "is"' (p. 10). Particularly significant has been the growing influence of ethos in debates associated with Schools Effectiveness and School Improvement (SESI). Bragg and Manchester point to the significant body of literature that suggests that there a clear link between school ethos and school effectiveness (Mortimore, 1988; Thacker and McInerney; 1992, Glover and Law, 2004). A particular concern is with how ethos may improve schools in areas of socio-economic deprivation or with disadvantaged populations (Gaziel, 1997; Strahan, 2003; Muijs, 2004). They cite Morris' (1995, 1998) observations that on Ofsted criteria, Catholic secondary schools provide a statistically significant higher standard and quality of education than others in the maintained sector. Other researchers suggest that culture or ethos is able to mitigate or mediate the effects of other educational practices or characteristics such as ability grouping (Hallam, 2004) or school size (Opedenacker, 2009).

Given Creative Partnerships was a high-profile, government-funded programme and for much of its lifespan, Arts Council branded, along with the focus it had on working in areas of deprivation, 'ethos' as it is currently conceived is clearly a topic of interest.

Types of creative school ethos

Through the Bragg and Manchester research the features of creative school ethos were developed under three single-word headings: considerate, convivial and capacious. These are not 'catch-all', comprehensive descriptions, however: they are inflected in particular ways that helped CCE explore significant aspects of practice. Each 'type' of ethos is summarised briefly below.

Considerate school ethos

One of three particular sorts of ethos within Creative Partnership schools was summed up by the term **'considerate'**. For Bragg and Manchester this referred to:

> [...] appropriate kinds of care, discipline and relationships in school, empha-
> sizing the importance of mutual, reciprocal civility, fairness and sensitivity,
> of safety and intelligibility. Being considerate might feature in definitions

of inclusive culture, but it is stronger than 'tolerance'. Thus it stresses more strongly the need to respect students' cultures and life experiences (which are often very different – and tougher – than teachers', especially in disadvantaged areas). (p. 7)

In such schools, children's lives and cultures beyond the school gates are respected and celebrated and are generally regarded as offering a positive addition to their school-based learning or to a creative process. Being considerate was about building an atmosphere in which students felt their views were heard and where they felt they mattered.

Creative Partnerships' supported this type of considerate school ethos through the following kinds of action:

- its commitment to youth voice, involving young people in decisions previously deemed to be beyond them, in different relationships with teachers and other adults;
- improving the material environment of a school, therefore catering for students' diverse and aesthetic needs and helping students feel 'cared for' and considered;
- additional funding for projects through which students feel valued, appreciated and noticed;
- extending extra-curricular provision to cater for a wide range of interests;
- supporting particular groups that are often invisible or overlooked so that they 'matter' and demand consideration, e.g. by controlling important resources, having work publicly displayed;
- valuing skills beyond the cognitive in creative projects;
- using artist resources to document learning and change displays, valuing students' work, rather than showy but static exhibits;
- encouraging reflective practice and ensuring it is built into projects;
- helping schools in disadvantaged areas to give positive accounts of their work and helping students to feel more positive about their association with the school.

Convivial school ethos

The second of the three types of ethos found to be most associated with Creative Partnerships was termed **'convivial'**. This type tended towards an emphasis on aspects of fun and enjoyment in learning and particularly the notion that teachers and students can enjoy being sociable and, as Bragg and Manchester put it, 'take pleasure in each others' company' (p. 11). This form of ethos also placed an emphasis on 'inter-dependence, interrelatedness, our reliance on others for identity and agency' (p. 12) and so suggested that schools where a premium was placed on social relationships had built the foundations for successful teaching and learning. Finally, it suggests an emphasis on inter-woven, contextual learning, often expressed by an integrated curriculum where facts and curriculum content connect with the wider world.

Bragg and Manchester found evidence that Creative Partnerships supported convivial school ethos through:

- 'offering students (sometimes comparatively rare) enjoyable and sociable experiences in its projects;
- legitimising partnership working, collaboration and mutually supportive relationships between teachers;
- challenging traditional hierarchies and role allocations;
- providing training on established approaches such as Forest Schools, which stimulate collective endeavour;
- [implementing] projects in which teachers and students both participate as learners and share feelings and ideas;
- respecting student cultures and knowledges in creative work;
- connecting students with networks beyond the school;
- supporting specific whole-school consultation events.' (p. 14)

Capacious school ethos

Finally, the **'capacious'** school ethos refers to the kind of liberating approach creative teaching and learning can foster and in particular the space-making aspects, allowing learning to range widely, both physically and mentally. The school itself may be seen as one of many learning sites and contexts, and so what Bragg and Manchester term 'a porousness' develops between school and community. It also refers to an increased attention to the use of physical learning spaces and the value of the aesthetic in class-rooms and communal areas.

Bragg and Manchester suggest Creative Partnerships supported capacious school ethos through:

- projects that improve and enrich the environment of school;
- enhancing expertise about the significance and meaning of the environment: for instance, through the creative practitioners employed and through it supplies;

- providing spaces where students and teachers can expand their sense of who they are allowed to be;
- supporting reflection on time as well as space in debates about the creative curriculum;
- acknowledging difference, drawing on creativity discourses that tend to value diversity above conformity.

While Creative Partnerships can be said to have helped to inculcate the values underpinning the three types of ethos described above, inversely, it is also likely to be the case that schools which have already developed these sorts of ethos will gain the most from creative approaches. It is worth, therefore, considering your own school or schools you may have worked in, and reflecting on whether one more than other descriptions approximates to your own context. Which of those, if any, comes closest to describing the learning environment you are already operating in or familiar with? How might the current ethos of your own school best be summarised? Is the school interested in developing a different approach to teaching and learning? Or perhaps is already well placed to make more use of creative partners and creative learning?

The School Ethos Research Project: Case studies of how types of ethos evolved in schools

To help situate the kinds of ethos Creative Partnerships helped evolve, and to bring these values to life in more explicit ways, the remainder of this chapter will offer some concrete examples from schools who were involved in the programme and took part in the CCE commissioned School Ethos Research Project. Bragg and Manchester provided an anonymised breakdown of the schools in brief terms in the final report as follows (2011, p. 27):

School	Context	Creative approaches	Creative Partnerships programme
Lange Nursery Inner-city estate nursery school co-located with a Children's Centre (ages 3–4). Ofsted: 'outstanding'	Transient, minority ethnic population. Stable staff. NOR: 71[4]	Long term, day-to-day relationships with creative practitioners (including an artist in residence). Reggio and Forest School approaches taken on as appropriate. Projects focused on environmental change and development of the school.	School of Creativity. Five years work.* Resident artist also on governing body.

School	Context	Creative approaches	Creative Partnerships programme
Delaunay Primary Inner-city nursery and primary school (ages 3–11). Global linking project with Pakistan and Lebanon. Ofsted: 'outstanding'	Transient minority ethnic population, plus children more settled in the local area. Stable staff. NOR: 230	Two artists in residence. Reggio and Forest School approaches in early years. Creativity related to global citizenship and the school's international linking projects with Pakistan and Lebanon.	School of Creativity. Six years work. School Creative Agent/ resident artist key partner at school. Creative Partnerships cluster leader.
Matisse School Special high school (ages 11–18). Specialist in cognition and learning. Co-located with a mainstream high school in a newly built 'education village'. Ofsted: 'outstanding'	Stable staff Very diverse student body with a range of needs. NOR: 100	Long term work with creative practitioners, focused on/in a multimedia suite. Creativity linked with wider inclusion, multimedia approaches and music technology.	No affiliation. Three years funded work. Not awarded School of Creativity status but continues to work with creative practitioners.
Sherman Secondary School Catholic Technology and applied learning college (ages 11–16) Outstanding Ofsted	Stable staff. Over subscribed, popular school. Good discipline. NOR: 728	Creative Partnerships co-ordinator central to the work. Some big projects with local arts organisations, and smaller-scale collaborations between creative practitioners and individual teachers, designing new teaching and learning strategies or schemes of work.	School of Creativity. Three years work. New Creative Agent. Work with feeder primaries.
Warhol School Inner-city secondary School, specialist humanities college (ages 11–16). OFSTED: 'outstanding' (received towards the end of our research period).	98% Muslim population, high staff turnover. Recent substantial improvement in exam results. NOR: 825	Creative Partnerships co-ordinator works closely with a creative agent. Creative practitioners work with a student 'youth panel' who are 'creative leaders' in school, and with selected teachers. Various environmental projects including graffiti murals, and a 'global garden' area designed by an artist working with teachers.	Change School. Two years work. 'Youth panel' present at local events etc.

* In this table, the 'years of work' given here refer to the number of years the school had been funded to run Creative Partnerships projects.

Using a range of fieldwork techniques the researchers combined different sets of data, including among others: student journals and sketchbooks, mapping the way spaces were used in school and photo voice (a technique whereby students depict their school's ethos in six defining images). This gave a rounded picture of the ethos in each school and helped build the final typology. In the examples that follow the intention is to show helpful parallels to the you that will inform your own reflections and development of your practice.

Examples of considerate school ethos

As briefly suggested above, considerate schools offer nurturing contexts in which to learn, where thought is put into issues of well-being for both staff and students. How is this manifest? Thoughtfulness and care tend to be manifest through the qualities of human interactions and relationships and these tend to be promoted through mutually agreed and understood behaviour codes, rather than through strategies for punishing non-conformist behaviour. There may be something particular about the ways creative professionals work with young people that accelerates and promotes this kind of ethos, as I hope to show later when we turn to consider the particular kind of value they may add.

In Sherman Secondary School it was noteworthy how rarely the researchers on School Ethos Research Project heard raised voices – as they had in many other schools – and they were struck by what seemed a standard mode of relaxed, courteous and respectful address between adults and young people. The researchers noted that pupils felt the boundaries were clear and that they knew 'where the line was'. Bragg and Manchester note that:

> Alongside this approach to discipline, a strong support system was provided, for instance, friendship and bereavement groups where, according to the head teacher, young people were 'encouraged to be mutually supportive of each other'. (p. 47)

Schools will always vary in the degree they look beyond basic legal responsibilities to ensure a physically safe environment and considerate schools were mindful of this. Students in the Creative Partnerships case-study schools involved in the School Ethos Research Project regularly reflected on their environment as a measure of their own value. How their learning environment was designed, in their view, said something about how high or low those that ran the school held them in esteem. As Bragg and Manchester point out:

Areas that were colourful, clean or appropriate signified that they were cared for, that they were being taken into account; but those that were dirty or smelly (typically, student-dominated areas such as particular corridors and toilets) marked the opposite. (p. 48)

The considerate ethos also extends to thought for learners' physical and psychological needs. At Lange Nursery, for example, the three and four year olds had become accustomed to the ringing of a bell at the end of a free play session that indicated it was time to sit down in 'family' groups. Understanding this pattern meant children were happier to participate in calmer sessions, on the understanding that there would be more 'up time' later in the day. The degree of attention given to bodily and emotional needs in the nursery was noteworthy for the researchers, particularly in contrast to secondary contexts that tended to relegate them to a position of low importance or even ignore them altogether. As Bragg and Manchester noted from their fieldwork:

[...] the pattern of the day was also logical; lunch was preceded by group time and massage, during which the intensity of earlier playing (and potential disputes) could recede. During massage time, calming music played, and the children – sitting in family groups – would each first ask permission and then massage one another. (p. 53)

The considerate ethos also extended to issues of safety and emotional security. A Year 11 pupil at Sherman described that at school students had a sense that there would always be someone appropriate to talk with about any pressing concerns. Many pupils at Sherman could name a favourite place in the school, places where they felt they could rest, relax and take time for themselves in an otherwise busy school day. At Delaunay Primary, children emphasised the help available from other children and staff at lunch or break times. At Lange Nursery, special attention was paid to moments of arrival and departure; key staff made themselves available to children and their parents, a chance to exchange news, update on progress or book a private time to discuss matters. Creative practitioners also engaged in discussion with parents at this time.

How Creative Partnerships contributed to the considerate school ethos

- Creative Partnerships' commitment to youth voice helped make student views more central to school processes, and involved young people in contexts and situations where they are treated with different kinds of courtesy and 'trusted', for instance to make decisions previously seen as beyond them. New documentation that Creative Partnerships introduced in 2008 stressed that schools should include young people in positions of governance, in planning and evaluating personalised learning and in relation to school environment and resources. Many Creative Partnerships schools involved young people in curriculum development and delivery; giving them a role in 'staff learning and development'; and in conceiving 'environment and resources' in imaginative ways that promoted discussion of learning spaces.

- Creative practitioners and creative approaches influenced the material environment of a school and therefore how far students felt 'cared for' and considered. Students at Sherman and Warhol School commented appreciatively on efforts to improve the environment, for instance where artists had designed artworks to distinguish between different subject areas or to decorate the school's toilets, or where artists had worked with young people to create a sculpture, a new garden area or a mosaic in outside areas. Young people claimed that such work 'affected their mood', and felt that it provided evidence that they were valued and that their needs and requirements were appreciated and being met.

- Creative Partnerships provided additional funding allowing schools to work on projects that often involved working in smaller groups, with concentrated periods of time given to projects, and less need to adhere to curriculum and teach for examinations. They could thus offer the kinds of reciprocal, inclusive relationships that are harder to achieve, particularly in secondary schools, where creative practitioners were freer to engage with young people's own concerns, experiences and interests. Some schools designed 'special attention' projects to prevent particular members of the school feeling overlooked: for instance, a secondary school sought out 'invisible' students – those who neither excelled nor misbehaved spectacularly – recognising that they were often overlooked.

- In some cases, Creative Partnerships funding supported specific student groups to gain in confidence, challenge presumptions and demand they be considered. For instance, in one setting, a group of students with disabilities were trained up to manage and use visual and audio equipment, thereby becoming the first port of call and an essential resource for anyone wanting to record school events or projects.

- Similarly, staff at Matisse School commented that one benefit of working in partnership with professional creative practitioners was that they enabled their students to produce work for display in public arenas – a contribution to ensuring young people with disabilities were considered, taken into account and mattered.

- Creative Partnerships' work brings outside professionals into school whose own working culture may be at odds with the school's – particularly schools that aim to enforce hierarchical consensus and consistency. For instance, it was common for artists to address students as they would any other client group, or as artists on a level with them. Students described this as making a difference to how they felt: a Year 9 boy who had worked with two creative practitioners on a youth governance project wrote in a diary entry that:

  The relationships between adults and young people are completely different. Nicola and David are like friends or colleagues. This creates a much better atmosphere to work in, ideas flow more freely because you aren't afraid of voicing your opinions. You know that whatever you say will be considered.

- Involvement in and evaluation of Creative Partnerships projects can help schools and teachers to reconsider their own relationships with young people – especially where they are used to more rigid and authoritarian ones. In reflecting on a school radio station set up by a creative media practitioner working with a small group of young people, the senior management team in a secondary school commented in an evaluation document that they became 'aware that we needed a level and trusted playing field with appropriate power structures and teachers and students. We felt that neither side should expect only to be heard, but also to hear.'

- Other examples of included Creative Partnerships funding being used to boost extra-curricular provision and increase students' feelings of being recognised or valued included the establishment of a school orchestra (called a 'Rawchestra') at Matisse School. It differed from a traditional school orchestra firstly, in being open to all: no previous experience of playing an instrument was required, and adults entered the project as learners alongside young people. Secondly, it developed pieces from ideas that members bought to the meetings. So in one session, a boy from Somalia sang a song from his home country and another brought in some lyrics that he had written at home. Creative practitioners worked with the Rawchestra to arrange these pieces for the instruments (using both assistive technologies and traditional instruments) that the adults and young people chose to play.

- When creative projects adopt a mode of working that does not focus on academic capabilities such as reading and writing, or speaking in certain (adult focused) ways, projects can make 'visible' different aspects of both students and teachers in a school. A Year 1 teacher suggested that a drama project supported by Creative Partnerships provided her with, 'a real chance to see [her students] being more creative, having this opportunity to be more relaxed and then seeing a side to them that you wouldn't see in a normal lesson.' At Delaunay Primary, the dance artist involved felt that giving children 'the opportunity to work together and be excited about creating movement and sculptures with their bodies' enabled them to support each other in ways that were sometimes difficult verbally'. He felt that this was especially the case where children did not speak English as a first language or lacked confidence orally.

- Creative Partnerships' activities may be precisely the kind of 'extra-curricular' provision that enable schools to give positive accounts of themselves, and that demonstrate caring about the well-being of young people rather than only about their examination results, which can turn a school's reputation around (Thomson et al., 2009). The desire to advertise these stories is not necessarily about being publicity-hungry: one student who remarked that ending up at a particular local ('hard') school was a sign that your parents did not love or care about you, revealing some rather more pressing reasons for changing the 'meaning' of a school. In one secondary school the deputy head narrated how projects organised by their creative agent – a school radio station and a youth led street dance performance – enabled them to turn around the negative image they had previously held in the local area after newspaper stories reported their success.

- When evaluating Creative Partnership programmes, young people frequently mentioned liking to see their own work displayed in communal and in classroom areas, and were dismissive of showy but static teacher-produced exhibits. Having creative practitioners in school to function as an additional resource and as someone skilled and confident about visual/aesthetic approaches, made it possible for displays to change more regularly and provide young people with a sense of being valued and 'seen', rather than invisible and overlooked. At Lange Nursery, staff documented activities on a daily basis through taking photographs and collecting children's work (whether 'finished' or not, and including all children rather than only 'best' work). A key task of the artist in residence was to collate and put this up in public areas every day, so the displays changed regularly. Children were often found looking at and talking about these together, delighting in pointing themselves out to adults (parents and staff), which often generated discussion around what they had done, and what they had enjoyed or disliked about the activity. The displays thereby became an important focus point for reflection. This approach to documentation and display both recognises the interest that parents have in their children's learning lives and the children's active participation in their own learning.

- Creative Partnerships as an organisation has consistently asked creative practitioners and teachers to build reflective structures into their projects, and have acknowledged the need to provide time for reflection and dialogue between teachers and artists, and between artists/teachers and young people. For instance its evaluation criteria for projects requires creative agents to hold beginning, midpoint and endpoint conversations with teachers, creative practitioners and young people taking part. It also encourages teachers and creative practitioners to identify an 'enquiry question' (as we have seen in Chapter 1) at the start of their collaboration thereby encouraging them to become action researchers, stepping back from their own practice to reflect on and learn from it.

Examples of convivial ethos in schools

Creative Partnerships schools provided many opportunities for fun lessons, active learning through mutual interest and thus developed a great deal of 'emotional engagement' between teachers and students. Through joint planning, reflecting and evaluating there opened up chances for everyone to offer something and make contributions that were treated as valid and worthwhile. This openness to ideas and suggestions is perhaps the hallmark of what Bragg and Manchester termed the 'convivial' ethos, a basic, positive and purposeful sense of camaraderie that united all participants in Creative Partnerships projects when they were working most effectively.

This sense of unity and equality of learning, where teachers are as much a part of the learning journey as students, gives rise to what Bragg and Manchester called a 'democratic perspective on the child's acquisition of knowledge and learning', recognising that the process is most effective when it is premised on 'creating knowledge together'. For example, at Lange Nursery, there was a great deal of freedom about choices of task and time spent on each activity; staff facilitated learning by participating with pupils in activities; staff noted what children did and what they enjoyed in order to inform future planning. Such approaches are often found in Early Years and Primary settings, where tracking and observation of learning is core to teacher's practice. As children get older, and as the transfer of knowledge via the curriculum begins to dominate it becomes more difficult to track learner development in quite the same way. In our experience, and as I hope to show in more detail in subsequent chapters, there was something particular about the ways creative practitioners worked, especially with older children, that re-opened those forms of assessment more associated with younger learners.

Delaunay School took on many pupils that had already been excluded from other schools in the area. They included, as Bragg and Manchester describe:

> *an eight-year-old boy described by the head teacher at his previous school as 'feral, lazy and difficult to control', and a ten-year-old boy who was the youngest person in the area to receive an Anti Social Behaviour Order (ASBO). (p. 39)*

Yet the school had considerable success in enabling both boys to achieve and to integrate. The school's ethos allowed for a 'fresh start' for each boy – only a select few teachers were made aware of the boy's prior history and there was a conscious decision to not label (and thereby limit) their potential to be positive members of the school community. Importantly, the ethos of the school allowed these new children to find their way into learning in the way that most suited them, without disrupting the learning of their peers. As Bragg and Manchester explain:

> *[...] the 'feral' child turned out to be one who hated to sit and listen, but could cope well if he was allowed the time he needed to play and explore. That is, his identity was not fixed but nor was it only up to him to change it: it depended on others, on the context, on how he was addressed, on how his behaviour was interpreted and on the breadth of responses and behaviours allowed him.(p. 40)*

A convivial ethos also seemed significant in relation to staff retention. The potential for Creative Partnerships work to offer a solid foundation for staff development will be discussed later in Chapter 5, but it is telling that within the context of school ethos, it was seen to be a key area of benefit. The 'convivial' sense of open and ongoing discussion helped to sustain teachers' professional dialogue and practice.

How Creative Partnerships contributed to the development of a convivial ethos in schools

- Creative Partnerships projects were generally felt to be exciting and enjoyable. At Lange Nursery the children were very enthusiastic about working with a storyteller. This enjoyment that was captured in the researcher's field notes:

  > When the children came out of the space they were all very enthusi-
  > astic – many of them wanted to tell the other staff and children in the
  > nursery about it. The resident artist videoed two boys trying to explain
  > about 'Billy Boat Buff' and resorting to showing what happened through
  > actions as they felt unable to express it in words. A little girl came out
  > saying, 'I been with John…that's John' and then started to re-role-play
  > the story with some plastic animals in the nursery.
  >
  > (Bragg and Manchester, Field notes, January 2010, p. 41)

- Creative Partnerships projects offered an alternative from some of the hierar-chical, negative and impersonal relationships experienced elsewhere in the school – between adults and young people and even among students. A female student at Warhol School commented how 'Sally (the artist) helps us a lot and we help each other.'
- Creative Partnerships offered teachers opportunities for enjoyment, stimu-lation and inspiration intrinsically – through the projects themselves, working alongside pupils and artists as co-learners – but also through Continuing Professional Development. An example of this was noted at Delaunay Primary where teachers worked with creative practitioners to make a collaborative sculpture to reflect on issues in education, and discuss their own inspirations and hopes for the future of the profession.
- 'Creative' approaches modelled by artists and other practitioners as part of the Creative Partnerships programme may have had a legitimizing effect on forms of partnership working and thereby encouraged greater levels of collaboration.

In one of the primary schools involved in the ethos study, teachers began planning lessons together, often repeating approaches that specific Creative Partnerships projects had used.

- Creative Partnerships often introduced alternative approaches to looking at practice and noticing learning and this recalibrated the teacher-pupil relationship in many ways, usually stopping it from feeling quite so hierarchical. Practitioners' influences often allowed teachers and other staff to be cast in roles as learners too and be perceived as such by pupils and peers. A visual artist at Delaunay Primary, for example, introduced the school's teaching assistants to a range of strategies for 'creative documentation' of learning which they took back into the classes they worked in. This gave the teaching assistants some key knowledge and new skills to share with their link teachers, who were then able to put the new knowledge into practice.
- One staff member in a Creative Partnerships school described to Bragg and Manchester the relationships involved in the more child-centred approaches her school had begun to take through their work with artists:

> It's about being brave enough to say to kids, '....I wonder if we could get our heads together and think of something that would cover all that [required content], commit to changing the way in which we learn. And I have an idea that if we were to do something about growing an outside garden which could help us look at some of the science of that, measuring things out, talking about the processes, then that might be a way forward and I wonder if anybody's got any ideas about how we can bring that together?'.
>
> (p. 49, cited in Bragg, Manchester and Faulkner, 2009)

- Creative Partnerships often worked well in conjunction with the Forest School approach, a way of learning which also places a premium on the social and emotional aspects of learning. One Forest School trained teacher at Delaunay Primary School combined the outdoors approach with some creative cooking by building a fire pit and cooking nettle soup with three year olds in the nursery; they first picked the nettles themselves (having been shown how to do so safely without gloves) before building the fire with the teacher. This culminated with the whole group sitting around the fire, sharing the soup – another example of how the bonding and sharing made possible through creative work can help facilitate learning.

- A different project, this time led by an artist at Sherman School, offers a further example of how the kind of ethos Creative Partnerships supported enabled emotional engagement and reciprocal learning. A Year 7 boy, thinking about the self-portrait he had created as part of the project, described feeling like he had 'weights on his shoulders' as he was expected to take on more responsibilities as he grew older; another girl created a 'masked' self portrait and explained her sense of having to put on a mask when she came to school. Interestingly, the teacher showed her own ghost-like portrait and explained that teaching was a performance where she, too, often thought she wasn't the same person she was outside of school.

- In Warhol School, some of the pupils reflected on how a Creative Partnerships project incorporating the skills of a textile artist gave them increased options about how to approach tasks, to take risks and experiment:

  […] she shows us how she does it first, and then we get to choose how we want to do it…(she) allows us to be creative learners – to get up, learn how you want to learn, feedback, help each other, make things, make mistakes and it doesn't matter. (p. 49)

- Creative Partnerships facilitated new contacts and collaborations with a range of differently skilled adults in the wider community – such as the police, social workers, youth workers, local councillors and other artists.
- A particularly effective way of modelling creative skills and behaviours was apparent at one Creative Partnerships school where former students who had since developed careers as professional artists came back to the school and offered to the students some very real and specific examples of bridging the world of school and creative work.
- Another particularly effective way Creative Partnerships offered a positive form of 'bridging' different worlds and senses of 'self' was found in projects that offered opportunities for students to bring aspects of their own lives into school. This was through the perennially popular media projects that enabled reflection on diverse issues such as peer pressure, consumerism and gang culture. At Matisse School, creative media practitioners were able to help draw on the students' cultural lives outside school, for example, through utilizing media forms such as scratching, mash-ups and video games in their lessons.

Examples of 'capacious' school ethos

This notion of a 'capacious' ethos was suggested by Bragg and Manchester as a way of signalling what might be thought of a 'space-making' opportunities afforded by the Creative Partnerships programme. It stemmed from the nature of the projects which were both planned collaboratively, but open to revision and adaptation – thereby affording a greater range of options, more room for manoeuvre, and a sense that pursuing a shifting horizon or revising multiple attempts to solve problems, for example, is a core part of the experience rather than a cause of confusion or stress. This particular school ethos encapsulates the conditions and frame of mind necessary to live with doubt, embrace uncertainty and manage fear of failure. As well as referring to the notion of room for doubt and alternatives in a cognitive sense, it also signifies the ways in which the learning spaces in education are influenced by creative practice, through aesthetics and an increased sensitivity to the material environment. This is undoubtedly an area where Creative Partnerships had significant impact.

Lange Nursery made use of Creative Partnerships as a means of completely redesigning the school interior, opening up rooms and creating larger spaces by removing partition walls. Despite having recently been given an 'outstanding' rating by Ofsted, Lange decided to move ahead with these dramatic changes anyway – this was rationalised as a sign of the ongoing commitment the school showed to continual reflection, based on Creative Partnerships principles of planning, reflection and evaluation, as to what works or is less effective for learners. The notion of change, and an environment that provided fresh stimulation, was versatile and open to ongoing change and rearrangement, all seemed to be vital to the school, despite having attained such a positive Ofsted report.

At Delaunay Primary, children displayed a great deal of confidence that seemed to stem from their sense of agency within the school environment. Other visitors from external organisations and new teachers also noted their generosity of spirit and high levels of confidence. Their desire and ability to ask questions was particularly noteworthy – they seemed to be very outward looking and brought to their conversations what felt like a deep-rooted curiosity. On the matter of the school playground redesign day they readily engaged in conversation with architects and builders about their ideas for a new outdoor space.

The resident artist at Lange Nursery also described a high level of agency amongst the three and four year olds who moved freely around the whole building, inside and outside. They were confident in approaching adult visitors to the school and were curious enough to ask many questions. The artist reflected on their ability to bring inquiring mindsets to all kinds of activities and remain deeply engaged in something even if it was just watching practice. This ubiquitous capacity for questioning and inquiry is a strong facet of individual creative learning and is clearly supported by a creative ethos in schools.

Capacious schools encourage a vantage point on issues affecting learning and topics within the curriculum that allow difference and applaud variety instead of demanding a one-size-fits-all approach. The male dance artist who worked with Delaunay Primary is a good example of this principle. He was selected by the school partly to feed into this overarching aspect of the school's ethos, as they looked to acknowledge and celebrate difference; he noted that part of his own satisfaction from working in the school stemmed from the children being allowed to be eccentric, rather than 'standardised or streamed'.

Delaunay Primary and Lange Nursery evidently embraced the need for a multiplicity of strategies in order to maximise children's potential to learn. In both settings learning was based on a strong spirit of inquiry and was purposefully unpredictable. It asked a lot of the teachers, requiring them to be attuned to a wide array of indicators of learning in children. The head teacher at Lange Nursery was unequivocal about the benefits that this open-ended approach to learning afforded young people:

> We want to allow children to be curious. And if they're curious they can do more for themselves. There's a range of ways of being involved and children will find their own route and their own way and if they develop confidence in an aspect then that will lead them onto something else. It's quite natural for some children not to like some things as much as others and that is quite acceptable.
>
> (Bragg and Manchester, p. 53)

Staff at Lange Nursery were committed to the idea that children's prior experiences and ongoing out-of-school experiences which they brought with them to nursery were a foundation on which to build new learning journeys. A small example of this is manifest through the teachers' responses to the children's improvised playing with 'junk modelling' resources, particularly cardboard tubes, which they began to look through as if they were telescopes or binoculars. The teachers went with this impromptu interest and developed a focus on 'different ways of seeing'. As Bragg and Manchester describe:

> *Staff began with a mind-mapping exercise, introduced them to artists such as Andy Goldsworthy and Yann Arthus-Bertrand and even climbed to the tops of tall buildings in the city, so that children could take birds-eye and eye-level photographs. (p. 56)*

As will have been evident from the examples above, 'capacious' schools are outward facing, treating the school gates as a potential conduit to new learning, rather than a way of shutting out distractions and non-school influences. In Creative Partnerships schools this manifest itself through diverse practices:

> *[...] such as young people working with children from feeder primaries, or with professionals from outside school; an emphasis on applying learning in different contexts and real-life situations; inviting people in to experience the school and share their expertise, making different kinds of connections with parents (beyond parents evenings) and with wider (including global) communities outside of school.*
>
> (Bragg and Manchester, p. 57)

At Matisse School children and staff from a partner primary school were trained in the filming techniques, taking their knowledge from a different context and thereby strengthening it. Opportunities for learners to teach the new skills they are acquiring is a common strategy in Creative Partnerships schools and is one way children are able to inculcate creative ways of thinking and doing.

This ability to explain how and importantly, why you have chosen to take an idea in a particular direction, or use particular sets of skills or resources is, in some ways, linked with the culture of planning and reflection that Creative Partnerships attempted to develop through the programme nationally. It encourages all participants in the programme to articulate a rationale as to why things might be done a certain way, which helps develop a common language of reflection. The resident artist at Lange Nursery captured the essence of this very clearly: 'Having had a number of visitors over the years we've had to articulate what we're doing and why and why it's important to us. That's helped everybody – particularly in terms of staff development and confidence.'

At Delaunay, this commitment to seeing value in articulating why things were done in a particular way and how they linked to specific outcomes came about through the completion of planning forms for the programme and engaging with research: 'My thinking, my vision, my values and my understanding of what we're about and where we want to go have been encapsulated – the journey that we're taking has become intrinsic to my way of thinking.' (p. 62)

How Creative Partnerships contributed to capacious ethos in schools

- Young people in Creative Partnerships projects often talked in terms of having created an alternative or parallel 'space'. This might be a literal redesigned learning space in a familiar classroom or a metaphorical space where they could expose themselves to risk, new ideas, taking chances and 'possibility thinking'. At Warhol School, a strict uniform policy was expected to be adhered to and the notion of flamboyance or expressivity was looked on with some scepticism by the predominantly 'laddish' youth culture. So a 'creative clinic' project that was designed to make learners more comfortable and relaxed about generating ideas and working spontaneously, utilised elaborately designed name badges and sets of brightly coloured fingerless gloves which were worn by the young people to signal that this space was different from the norm. They quickly acclimatised to the notion of things happening differently in that space and were soon working together to generate ideas and make their projects happen without requiring prompts from the teacher. All of this was starkly different from the more regimented ethos elsewhere in the school.
- Space could sometimes be transformed literally and dramatically, for example when Creative Partnerships was mobilised in conjunction with the Building Schools for the Future (BSF) programme. Delaunay Primary's early years team collaborated with the resident Creative Partnerships artist in ways that informed the BSF work, transforming the playground space to create an exploratory learning space where risk taking and testing of boundaries were actively encouraged. Again, this was in stark contrast to some of the out-of-school spaces the children were used to.
- Similarly the fences around Delauney Primary were decorated and re-designed to incorporate plastic pipes for experiments with water and included an interactive sound sculpture – a signal that the barriers separating school were permeable and a chance to continue experimenting and thinking beyond the school gates. Every chance to inculcate values of thinking, inquiry and questioning frames of mind were taken by the school and this was done within the context of connecting school with the wider world rather than setting the school up as a separate, 'other' or alternative space.

- Sometimes, unproductive or stale educational approaches can be fixed by time as well as structured by the physical spaces around the school. Creative Practitioners often helped to constructively disrupt the 'curriculum clock' resetting a rhythm that often found a cycle of its own, outside of the constraints of timetabled lessons. The staff at Delaunay Primary and the creative practitioners working with them openly reflected on how creative projects slowed down learning in some respects which contrasted with what Bragg and Manchester characterise as 'the pressures to "fit in" all of the curriculum that they often felt in the classroom'. (p. 49)

- In many areas, Creative Partnerships staff provided professional development based on Reggio Emilia and/or Forest School approaches, which encourage reflection on learning, integrated curriculum approaches, mixed ability teaching, learning about and in natural environments (and 'the environment as third teacher'), taking the lead from the child, following their interests, rather than delivering pre-packaged curriculum.

- One Creative Partnerships project involved a professional photographer taking family portraits of the children with their siblings, parents/carers. The project's intent was to look at collective ambition, sets of common goals that may help shape the young people's choices over the long term. Families would be photographed and summarise their hopes for the future in a short passage that would accompany the final image. The outcomes were a fascinating and rich insight into a hitherto unseen culture. One that challenged the myth of 'low aspirations' in poorer communities. The teachers were so surprised by the depth of ambition and aspiration that it led to a reappraisal around how the school might better support their children but also parents and the wider community. I will come onto consider in greater detail the ways Creative Partnerships can connect with parents in a later chapter.

- One of the main drivers for Creative Partnerships work was to help increase the capacity of teachers through long-term partnerships with creative practitioners. This would sometimes take the form of formal Continuing Professional Development sessions as well as access to participating in research. At Matisse School, the deputy head articulated the view that the experience of being within the Creative Partnerships programme had helped to develop a more authentic learning culture, one where teachers felt confident enough to try new things out, and to 'have a go' and where the 'stickability' of learning and professional development was enhanced partly by thinking over longer cycles of time in the way creative practitioners encouraged. A teacher working in a Creative Partnerships primary school, and reflecting on her peers, explained:

> *We are very open to new ideas and that ethos now goes throughout the school – that you can take a risk, you can have a go. If it doesn't work then you do it again, or you change it for next time. That's definitely one of the benefits of artists coming in.*
>
> (Bragg and Manchester, p. 56)

- At Sherman School, one teacher pointed towards a more capacious form of learning, arguing that creative approaches highlighted the benefits of, and discipline associated with, working from and with mistakes – 'developing it further and you work it and work it and work it.' This notion of extending learning through a process of ongoing refinement and reflection is one that seems to be central to creative practice and we shall return to this idea later.

This chapter has attempted to set out three particular types of school ethos, considerate, convivial and capacious, each one distinguished from the other in order to illustrate key points rather than suggest any strict division. Clearly they overlap and there is a relationship between them, and in the ways day-to-day teachers, artists and young people negotiated with each and helped to construct their schools' version of a creative ethos.

The key principle of this chapter is that in order to embrace creative learning across schools, or even within individual classrooms, an ethos of the sort described here is a great enabling force, and an asset to be acknowledged openly, and valued accordingly. If such an ethos does not already exist, then, the evidence from the Creative Partnerships programme suggests that the process of working creatively, especially where that can be done with creative partners from beyond the school, may well begin to establish one.

Having considered school ethos in some detail, we will now turn to the challenging issue of what impact such schools may or may not have on what for many external commentators and policy-makers is still the education system's bottom line – benefits for pupils, particularly around attainment.

4 Creative Learning – Pupil Impact

Creative Partnerships programmes had many ambitions, and among the most significant were improving learning outcomes for children. In this chapter, the key impacts on attainment and well-being will be described and some suggestions as to why they may have occurred will be developed. The key point here will be that creative approaches to education do not have to force an either/or choice between 'academic standards' and 'wider benefits' such as motivation, confidence or emotional literacy. There is evidence collected from Creative Partnerships suggest it is quite possible to have both.

It is notoriously difficult to pinpoint causal relationships between educational interventions and specific improvements in attainment. So many other factors come into play that it makes tying together inputs and outcomes in a simplistic way next to impossible. However, given the nature of Creative Partnerships and the fact that the programme was of a significant size and spread across large numbers of schools, it was possible to undertake the sorts of quantitative analysis creative and arts interventions are not ordinarily subjected to.

Before we go on to consider the ways in which Creative Partnerships programmes may have helped create more effective learning opportunities for young people we will first consider what the statistics suggested when it came to impact on attainment.

What the numbers say: statistical analyses of Creative Partnerships' impact on pupil attainment and attendance

In a programme of the size of Creative Partnerships, it will always be possible to find a handful of excellent examples of best practice, but it is another thing altogether to assert that such examples are indicative of the 'average' practice. One of the ways that Creativity Culture and Education (CCE) tried to keep an eye on the big picture, as well as individual case studies, was to commission research that analysed comparatively large data sets and looked for patterns that might have emerged as a result of

Creative Partnerships. While this kind of work is never a straightforward case for causal effects it did help by offering a counterbalance to one-off examples by showing the overall effects the programme may have had. These were usually much smaller in size and less dramatic than the accounts offered by qualitative narratives, but they still have a place in telling the story of impact.

Each year, from 2006 onwards, CCE undertook a statistical analysis that juxtaposed a range of different measures. CCE looked at the attainment of children in Creative Partnerships schools when compared to children from similar backgrounds in non-Creative Partnerships Schools; it looked at the attainment of children in Creative Partnerships schools in comparison to children in the same school who had not been involved in Creative Partnerships projects. CCE also looked at these in relation to national averages, and of course was able to look at effect sizes in different age ranges and between boys and girls.

At the same time, the National Foundation for Educational Research (NFER) conducted separate studies, looking at test results across a period of eight years (Sharp et al., 2006; Eames et al., 2006; Durbin et al., 2010; Kendall et al., 2008a and b; Cooper et al., 2011). Initially we were able to make use of pupil data, giving us the chance to make an analysis at the level of individual learners. This was made possible by the 'registers' that were kept during the earliest years of Creative Partnerships, identifying the individual pupils involved. The registers could not be sustained throughout the life of the programme as it was too burdensome for schools to do so. In the absence of registers the later statistical studies looked at shifts happening across the whole school, or by year group or gender, but not down at the level of the individual pupil.

The results of the analysis were very interesting, indicating the possibility of positive effects in significant numbers of young people, and this gave some support to the notion of a 'Creative Partnerships effect' at work in the range of projects happening across thousands of schools.

The studies were based on large samples of primary and secondary schools (around 400) and pupils (around 61,000). A 'virtual control group' design was used. The process is described by Sharp and Cooper (2012) as follows:

- Researchers identified which schools and individual young people had been involved in the initiative. The team asked all participating schools to identify which young people had taken part in Creative Partnerships activities each term.
- The team requested access to the National Pupil Database, held by the Department for Education. This comprises information on all English

pupils each year, including background characteristics and attainment. (The Department makes this available for research, under certain conditions.).

- The next stage was to identify a comparison group of similar schools, especially those serving disadvantaged backgrounds, and to locate the information on attainment and attendance for all pupils in the Creative Partnerships and comparison schools.
- The team constructed statistical models, to take account of prior attainment and individual characteristics known to affect outcomes (such as special educational needs, gender and economic disadvantage). They used a process known as multilevel modelling, to take account of data at different levels (e.g. the pupil and the school).
- Finally, the team interpreted the results, comparing progress within and between schools.

An analysis was undertaken at both school and pupil levels:

- School-level analysis: compared Creative Partnerships schools with other similar schools.
- Pupil-level analysis: compared pupils who took part in Creative Partnerships activities with those who did not, in the same schools.
- The results for the school-level analysis are shown in Table 1, reproduced from the CCE publication, *Changing Young Lives: Research Digest* (2012).

Years analysed	Positive impact on schools involved with Creative Partnerships				
	KS1:	KS2:	KS3:	KS4:	Area of better progress:
2003 2004			✓		Average score, mathematics, science
2005			✓		Average score, English, mathematics, and science
2006				✓	Total GCSE point score, best 8 point score, English and science
2007 2008				✓	Total GCSE point score
2009		✓			Average score, science
2010				✓	Total GCSE point score, capped points score

Table 4.1 The impact of Creative Partnerships on attainment at the school level

Table 4.1 sets out where positive associations between secondary schools taking part in Creative Partnerships and higher attainment were found for pupils at Key Stage 3 and 4 between 2003 and 2010. We also asked NFER to carry out pupil-level analysis. The results are shown in Table 4.2.

Years analysed	Positive impact on pupils involved with Creative Partnerships				
	KS1:	KS2:	KS3:	KS4:	Area of better progress:
2003 & 2004		✓			Average score, English, mathematics, science
			✓		Average score, English, mathematics, science
				✓	Total GCSE point score, best 8 point score, science
2005 & 2006		✓			Average score, English, science
			✓		Average score, English, mathematics, science
				✓	Total GCSE point score, best 8 point score, English, science
2007 & 2008	*school level analysis only*				
2009	✓				Speaking and listening
2010		✓	✓		Average, English, mathematics, science; (x = Key Stage 2 English)
	✓				average, speaking and listening, Reading, science
			✓		Average, English
				✓	Total GCSE point score, capped Points score

Table 4.2 The impact of Creative Partnerships on attainment at the pupil level

The results, again, are positive impacts, statistically significant, indicating that the attainment of young people who had taken part in Creative Partnerships had improved. Pupils attending Creative Partnerships made greater progress in national tests at Key Stages 1, 2, 3 and 4. The differences were between pupils taking part in Creative Partnerships activities and others, either in the same schools or in schools not taking part in Creative Partnerships.

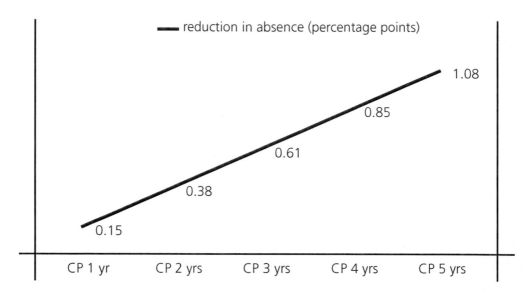

Figure 4.1 Absence rates for primary schools involved in Creative Partnerships for different lengths of time

An example of the difference that Creative Partnerships made to young people's learning in 2010 was that young people who attended Creative Partnerships activities achieved an average of one level higher in their Key Stage 3 average points score than expected, given their background characteristics.

The NFER also studied attendance rates in primary and secondary schools involved in Creative Partnerships. A study exploring attendance rates from 2003 to 2007 (Durbin et al., 2010) found a positive difference for primary schools which were involved in Creative Partnerships for several years. This is shown in Figure 4.1, again reproduced with permission *Changing Young Lives* (2012).

Creative Partnerships primary schools started with similar absence rates to one another (approximately 5%), rates that were also similar to the non-Creative Partnerships schools. However, over time as schools remained with the Creative Partnerships programme a trend emerged for the absence rates to fall. This was not the case for similar schools outside of the Creative Partnerships programme. As Sharp and Cooper (2012) point out: 'In statistical terms, an effect size of 0.25 is considered large enough to be *educationally significant* (Slavin and Fashola, 1998).' The graph above shows that this threshold was reached after just two years.

The most recent CCE-commissioned study looked at the effect of Creative Partnerships on student total absence (the combination of both authorised and unauthorised absence) and unauthorised absence (where no permission has been given by the school) in 2009 and 2010. The results are summarised below in Table 4.3.

Years analysed	Type of analysis	Impact on pupils involved with Creative Partnerships		
		Primary	Secondary	Effect
2009			✓	Minor reduction in total absence
2010	school and pupil level	✓		minor reduction in unauthorised Absence

Table 4.3 The impact of Creative Partnerships on attendance in 2009 and 2010

Here we see some minor falls in total absence at both school and pupil levels, but they were not consistently found in both phases of education over both years.

What these studies show very clearly is that, when a statistical analysis of available data was made, it indicated Creative Partnerships appeared to have had significant impacts for pupils. Pupils did better in assessments at Key Stages 1, 2, 3 and 4. And across the series of studies, secondary school students appeared to do best of all.

As well as the analysis of national data on attainment and attendance, other research CCE had commissioned revealed pupil impacts of a different sort. The study by McLellan et al. (2012) on the effects of Creative Partnerships on pupil well-being suggests there are some clear benefits to this way of working that may have profound effects on children's general disposition towards learning and their overall confidence and world-view.

The study found that schools observed within the Creative Partnership programme all tended to view creativity and creative learning as a way of actively developing student well-being – creativity was perceived by teachers and artists as an explicit process through which student well-being was improved. In contrast, schools observed with no Creative Partnership programme tended to use initiatives or projects as tools to support students learning in partial ways, so students were, for example, often removed from the class to participate in 'additional' activities and then be reintroduced into the 'normal' lesson later. As McLellan et al. (2012) point out:

> *This bolt-on approach led some students and staff to the realisation that this provision could be unfair – 'it's great here if you are naughty'. Creative Partnership schools tended to have a more inclusive approach. (p. 6)*

In the next section, we will move on to focus on this exploration of well-being, and thereby illustrate how creative learning can have significant impacts on pupils in relation to what might be called 'soft outcomes' as well as exams and tests.

Creativity and pupil well-being – how does a creative approach help?

The Creative Partnership programme was most successful in promoting pupil well-being where staff (and particularly senior staff) took a 'whole-school' approach to creative learning, giving it a value and credibility and creating expectations that all staff would be active in the programme. Under these conditions it was often the case that creativity was explicitly highlighted as important to school development rather than something that was an experiment, tolerated by the many and championed by the few. In a study by McLellan et al. (2012) all Creative Partnership schools observed were committed to long term engagement with creative approaches and these carried on between and after visits from creative practitioners. Where schools in the study without a Creative Partnership programme instigated creative approaches these were generally 'stand-alone', not integrated into a longer-term plan or high-level vision for the school. Such work tended to be located in after school slots or as rewards or 'special' work when the normal timetable was temporarily suspended. While children certainly enjoyed many of these less-integrated activities it was notable that there was little evidence that such experiences influenced classroom learning (McLellan et al., 2012, p.8)

As well as this holistic approach, another key enabling factor was the opportunity afforded by creative work to gain new skills and knowledge in authentic and enjoyable ways. A wide range of stimulating Creative Partnership activities were observed across the schools that took part in the Cambridge study. Activities were cross-curricular, mobilising a style of learning that fused subject areas and connected knowledge rather than dealing with each subject in turn. An emphasis was placed not only on artistic skills, but also on transferable skills such as working in teams and problem solving. This feature of Creative Partnerships – its ability to help make the curriculum seem more relevant, more holistic, and more interesting as a result – is echoed by other research, which we will look at in subsequent chapters.

Another key factor in promoting well-being was an element we have already touched on with reference to school ethos – the deep-rooted sense of collaboration that was a driving force at the heart of many Creative Partnerships activities. For example, projects would often focus on a joint outcome rather than on students' individual creations and these joint outcomes, while developing aspects of personal well-being also allowed the social dimensions of well-being to come to the fore. Pupils enjoyed the purposeful and positive feelings associated with working with others, and appeared to respond well to the notion of supporting and being supported.

Also prevalent in strong Creative Partnership projects was the emphasis placed on relationships developed between teachers and creative practitioners. A joint approach gave teachers the confidence to try new approaches to activities in a supported way while the practitioners were able to become part of the school, offering a more sustained engagement with the kinds of practice required to support creative learning.

Effects of creative approaches on student well-being

What might be the likely outcomes of creative projects on student well-being? Having described above some of the key features of successful projects in the Creative Partnerships programme that related to student well-being we can now briefly touch on the perceived effects that such projects had on students. What were the discrete impacts that may have influenced students' self-concept and given rise to a greater sense of well-being? CCE commissioned researchers from Cambridge University to take a detailed look at the effects of Creative Partnerships on pupil well-being and the following section draws on the main findings from their work

Student engagement

A sense of well-being is linked to a sense of purpose in learning contexts. It was noteworthy that when Creative Partnerships activities were observed by the research team there was a palpable sense that students enjoyed and were engaged in what they were doing. While this might seem a banal observation on one level – the fact that creative activities are more enjoyable to children is no surprise – it is interesting that a long-term change was also noticed by teachers, who frequently commented on the extent to which creative activities helped to engage those students who found particularly challenging the more structured classroom, where the mode of learning was based more on a model of transmission of facts rather than discovery of principles.

When asked for an initial response to what working on Creative Partnerships had been like for them, students would often invoke the notion of it being more 'fun'. Exploring this further during interviews with students, the researchers found that there were several aspects that seemed particularly important and these are summarised below.

The chance to make decisions

It was clear from the research that working with creative practitioners gave students many opportunities to make decisions about their own learning. Pupils commented on enjoying not being told what to do all the time, and having an increased sense of 'freedom' to learn through less structured 'trial and error' style activities. Some schools within the study had clearly transferred higher levels of student choice back into 'mainstream' lessons. There were examples of

> [...] students making decisions about what topics to explore, how to approach different tasks and taking responsibility for reflecting on learning. In other schools student decisions were confined to matters such as organising classroom space and choosing where to sit.
>
> (McLellan and Galton, 2012, p. 72)

Less formality in learning contexts

The working relationships between students and creative practitioners were described by researchers as 'informal and friendly'. This echoes the findings of the School Ethos Research Project by Bragg and Manchester (CCE, 2011), as seen in Chapter 3, in which they noted the positive effects of a convivial ethos underpinning creative learning. The artists and creative practitioners were less interested in controlling behaviour, achieving this indirectly through more open-ended approaches to learning, and there was very little by way of 'routines-and-procedures' type talk observed, limiting the sense of institutional authority and hierarchy and instilling a (creative) professional working atmosphere akin to an open studio space or workshop. The informal atmosphere in the Creative Partnerships projects often spilled over into 'normal lessons'. For example, students were less inclined to go out to play because work itself had become a sociable, friendly and playful activity.

More student voice present in and around the school

Again, and in concert with the School Ethos study previously described, McLellan et al.'s well-being study found practices associated with 'student voice' were evident within Creative Partnerships projects. With children and young people contributing to decisions about their own learning, evolving rules of behaviour and in some cases the recruitment of staff, there was a clear shift in the sense of agency they had in determining their learning environment. The researchers also noted that in schools which had a commitment to well-being, but with no Creative Partnerships projects, although there were formal procedures which allowed for student decision making, these often involved only nominal consultations (McLellan et al., 2011).

A flexible interpretation of the National Curriculum

The researchers found evidence that schools within Creative Partnerships had developed a more flexible approach to curriculum planning over their time within the programme. There was a strong emphasis on cross-curricular work. While in itself this may not have directly contributed to a sense of pupil well-being it is evident that such approaches to lateral planning, topic-based work and the ability to pursue a theme in ways that embrace multiple subject areas are all fertile conditions in which the other aspects mentioned above can flourish.

What difference did Creative Partnerships make to well-being in schools?

The research study by McLellan et al. explored approaches to well-being across a number of schools, some engaged with the Creative Partnerships programme and others that were not. The researchers summarised the key differences they felt were most sharply defined when comparing Creative Partnerships schools with the others they observed and the main contrasting elements are set out below:

- Creative Partnerships' approach to fostering well-being was markedly different from that in the other schools observed in the research study. In the latter, **well-being was a means to an end** in that various activities designed to make pupils feel better in themselves or to make them more confident were intended to overcome the low motivation levels which operated in core subjects such as literacy and mathematics. In Creative Partnership schools, there was no distinction made between creativity and well-being. As a result **creative learning tended to permeate the whole curriculum.**
- Pupils' voice was a crucial aspect in promoting well-being and in helping students to function effectively both personally and socially. **The extent to which pupils were able to have their views recognised and contribute to decision making had been taken further in the Creative Partnership schools**. In contrast, pupils in the other schools were often unaware of how their School Council operated or its remit.
- There were indications that the **superior scores of Key Stage 1 on the well-being scales could be attributed, in part, to Creative Partnership activities.**

The same was not true in the case of the Key Stage 2 sample, where pupils in the non-Creative Partnership schools did marginally better. The lower KS2 results may be attributed to the fact that the administration of the well-being survey coincided with preparation for SATs. Pupils said that the SATs caused both them and their teachers considerable anxiety.

- There was little evidence that creative learning was promoted through specific 'arts-based' approaches to learning. **In all Creative Partnership schools the emphasis was on generic pedagogies rather than pedagogic subject knowledge**. Specialist knowledge and skills were only introduced when it helped pupils to develop their own ideas. The emphasis was mainly to help students to think flexibly, strategically and creatively.

- **Creative Partnerships schools conceptualised creativity as a generic process** that is applicable in all subject areas, with a greater emphasis on creativity as a process than creativity as an outcome.

Impacts on student learning – the case of visual learning and literacy skills

So far in this chapter we have seen evidence that Creative Partnerships had an impact on academic performance and school attendance, as well as promoting a deep sense of well-being. The section that follows will look more closely at the impact of a particular form of creative learning – in this example, through the work of a visual artist – and show in a grounded sense how a specific creative medium can have the effect of boosting attainment in other areas.

In the early years of Creative Partnerships (2003/04) the renowned linguistic anthropologist Professor Shirley Brice Heath and her colleague Professor Shelby Wolf undertook a series of narrative studies of a single school in South East England. They followed the creative practitioners, in this case artists, for a whole academic year in Hythe Community School, describing in detail their methods and approaches, while looking for evidence of their impact on teaching and learning.

Brice Heath and Wolf looked at a range of visual art activities including drawing, clay work and the making and reading of picture books (2004) and described the ways in which such activities offered deeper understanding of concepts and improved verbal expression, boosting metaphorical analysis and narrative interpretation.

One artist they observed at work, Roy Smith, ran a series of sessions that were based on the concept of 'portraits'. The class began in a traditional way, discussing famous artists who had been known for their portrait painting – Van Gogh, Manet and Leonardo da Vinci. Roy then changed the focus of the lesson completely by moving from the perhaps rarefied and intimidating world of famous artists to the world of the individual learners in the class. He did this by distributing small, hand held mirrors to the class. He encouraged the students to begin to draw self-portraits but emphasised that they should try to do so by putting most effort and time into 'looking' into the mirrors rather than drawing. The idea was to subvert the usual reliance on memory and the mind's eye. Roy explained that good drawing was about being able to almost forget about the hand holding the pencil and concentrate instead looking closely at the image reflected in the mirror. This would help many students, who felt they had reached a 'plateau' in their ability to draw. Roy encouraged them to keep 'looking' and to try to draw from direct observation and not from memory.

An example of Roy's approach is captured well in this extract from an exchange with students part way through the self-portrait challenge:

> Roy: *Now, the next thing to do is draw the eyes. Now, are my eyes on the top of my head?*
> Children (giggling): *No! They're down there (pointing to their eyes).*
> Roy: *They're down there. If I measure it on my face, they're about half way. So halfway down my face is where I draw my eyes. And we'll draw them as long squashed circles, called ovals. Now you draw two ovals halfway down the head. Perfect Louis!*
> Louis: *Yeah!*
> Roy: *Next thing to do is notice the circle inside the eye's oval, because that's the iris. That's the part of your eye that has colour. What colour are your eyes? (…) Now inside the eye, if you look at the person next to you, is a black bit. There's a black circle called the pupil. We can make that nice and dark. Now we saw earlier that if you look at the eye (the iris) has little lines (inside it). So we can draw those lines in there. Matthew show us…*
>
> (Brice Heath and Wolf, 2004, p. 16)

Matthew was a boy in the class who, at the first attempt, seemed to sustain an interest in 'looking' and observing that bit more keenly than some of his classmates. Roy had noticed this and remarked on it. As a result of Matthew's sustained 'looking', he had observed fine lines radiating out from the pupil towards the outer ring of the iris and included them in his portrait. So Roy's talk with the class is both reinforcing the students' own artistic skills and abilities while demystifying his own practice

('Matthew show us' rather than 'Do as I say'). It is also peppered with constant reminders to look and take notice of detail – prompts to look into mirrors and at one another's faces.

Brice Heath and Wolf built a narrative over a year-long study to show how attention to the visual world at Hythe Community School helped develop better levels of verbal and written articulation. In a sense, their argument is about how reading and writing needs to be developed through more explicit links to its earlier forms of meaning based on pictures and inference. While observing teachers at work both with and without artists, a clearer picture of the kind of value added by artist and creative practitioners begins to emerge.

In another example from the same school, Brice Heath and Wolf describe how an activity based on the production of picture books led to children using metaphor and the interpretation of texts in ever more sophisticated ways. The start point for this work was the realisation that picture books are familiar to teachers, and emergent readers are used as a way of developing the habit of making meaning with books. There was a curiosity about picture books and the question of whether they were used to their fullest potential was in the teacher's minds.

In a discussion about picture books the Hythe teachers acknowledged that while 'the children are listening, they're looking at the pictures' too. But they wondered if this looking was as deep as it could be. Was the kind of precise and detailed look encouraged by Roy in his drawing work likely to be of use in the reading of visual texts? What kinds of interpretative choices would they make, now that they had developed a particular way of seeing objects in detail, with proper attention to colour, texture and shade. With these questions in mind, the teachers resolved to share picture books with their pupils in more complex and critical ways than before, exercising the new vocabularies they had begun to develop and to use this as a way of offering a deeper learning experience.

A good example of this process was the experience of a then trainee teacher, Marion Broom, who was on a practical placement at Hythe. She was keen to develop work with picture books. She was aware that she had her own preferences when it came to such books, enjoying detailed, complex illustrations that could hold several potential stories simultaneously. Through the Creative Partnerships work at Hythe, Marion was coming to a clearer understanding of why she liked particular sorts of book, and the dimensions within them that gave her a form of interpretive pleasure. One such book was the tale of Rufus O'Parsley in *The Rascally Cake* (Willis, 1995).[5] When the class of Year 2 children read this book with Marion they were delighted by the pictures of awful foods and liked the detail within the large illustrated pages. At the end of the story they asked to take a closer look at the pages and Marion placed the open book on the floor for them to huddle round.

> Marion: *Every time I look at this book, I find more in it – more details in the illustrations. Every time you read it you see something new.*
> Jack: *I saw that picture before. Look! Look! (Jack, flipping back between one of the early illustrations and the final image, shows the contrast between the glutton and the gourmet, with the perspective identical, but the details changed).*
> Marion: *But they're not the same are they?*
> Hannah: *No, they're not the same.*
> George: *They're not the same. Here he's got big long eyebrows.*
> Hannah: *Eeeeewwww. And there are snakes everywhere.*
> Jade: *It's like the snakes on the front cover*
> Jack: *And all that food. That's why he's so fat.*
> Hannah: *And he throws the bones on the floor.*
> Jack: *I never saw that before. Mrs Brook can I take that book home in my book bag?*
>
> (Brice Heath and Wolf, 2005, p. 36)

This realisation that there was more to see, more even than the afternoon reading session would allow, prompted Jack to see if he could take the book home. The time needed to spend looking, and the pleasure in noticing the detail and expressing it through reading or explanation, is something the researchers and teachers felt was directly derived from the way the school has prioritised visual art and visual learning. It increased the pleasure children took from reading and gave them the confidence to suggest what things might mean, rather than guess what 'correct' answer might already lurk inside a teacher's head. For many, this would serve as evidence of a deeper and arguably more authentic learning experience and would be an end in itself. But is there any impact on exams and tests when schools adopt creative approaches to teaching and learning?

Creativity, Culture and Education (CCE) commissioned a series of studies looking at statistical evidence of Creative Partnerships' impact on attainment and overall engagement with school. The National Foundation for Educational Research (NFER) undertook the studies (CCE, 2006, 2008a, 2008b, 2010) and used a technique known as multi-level modelling to attempt to isolate the 'CP effect'. The results were interesting. There were some positive relationships between attainment at Key Stages 3 and 4 and lower rates of fixed-term exclusions in both primary and secondary schools taking part in Creative Partnerships when compared to national averages. The studies also point to effects being felt strongest when the schools remained in the programme for longer periods, usually at least two years (Kendall, et al., 2010, p. 23). This suggests that the positive benefits associated with any new, exciting programme in schools during its initial stages (partly just because of its novelty) is backed up by a longer-lasting effect which may relate to the kinds of pedagogy illustrated above in the examples from Hythe school.

Summary: The outcomes of Creative Partnerships

The experience of Creative Partnerships suggests that there are varieties of impacts and effects that could occur as a result of implementing creative approaches to teaching and learning. Those most closely associated with students have been impacts on well-being, impacts on academic achievement and, although strongly linked with well-being, impacts on youth voice and the sense of engagement with the life of the school this can bring about.

The features that tie these impacts together are all clearly defined by particular pedagogical approaches that, in a number of ways, rebalance principles of teaching and learning in classrooms and all of these approaches could be applied in your school or teaching practice. Common to all the studies analysed for this chapter have been the following:

- An authentic and deep commitment to youth voice: an understanding that youth voice work at its best becomes a de facto commitment to joint planning, learning and reflecting, taking it beyond the sphere of more tokenistic manifestations of youth voice and into the realm of genuine co-learning where teachers, students and artists learn together.
- A child-centred approach to learning: ensuring the needs of the learner rather than the content of the curriculum are taken as the start point. Creative Partnerships schools, at their best, have used a teaching or learning issue or need as a way of mobilising creative learning, but they have not lost sight of the fact that creative skills and habits of mind are important outcomes in their own right.
- An approach to learning that is less about teacher transmission of facts and more about discovering for oneself through investigation or trial and error. This affords a heightened sense of personal achievement and certainly, from

the NFER findings, would not appear to adversely affect the business of passing exams.

- Teaching through modelling new and alternative practices; the examples used in all the studies cited here show that Creative Partnerships offered value to teachers and students by providing links to alternative ways of working as modelled by artists and creative practitioners. These ways of working model different sorts of teaching and learning behaviours that seem to have offered a more satisfying learning experience to young people.

In the chapter that follows we will explore the ways that teachers used Creative Partnerships as a means of professional development, and therefore, indirectly as a way of building an ecology within the school that would allow some of the conditions and outcomes described above to flourish.

5 Creative Professional Development for Teachers

Indirectly, Creative Partnerships was always about teacher development. The planning processes and partnership approach to delivering projects meant that teachers were engaged with new and different ways of thinking and delivering in relation to their pedagogy. In addition, there were explicit Continuing Profession Development (CPD) elements to the programme that aimed to develop teacher confidence and competence. What were the effects of this and what has been the legacy of this work for teachers now the national programme has ended?

There is a history of teachers working with artists and cultural organisations across the UK, most notably through art-form specific projects such as theatre-in-education, artists in schools programmes, visiting musicians and writers, and also collaboration with museums and galleries whereby school lessons or learning objectives are linked with specific collections or exhibitions. Typically this tended to be short term as it served as a means of superficially boosting enjoyment amongst pupils. However, the expertise seemed to reside almost exclusively with the external partners and there was no real strategy for long-term sustainability or for changing the culture of schools and teachers. Creative Partnerships, to an extent, was designed with this in mind, drawing on the many evaluations of such work that called for long-term relationships and more sustained partnerships to be formed between schools and creative and cultural people and organisations.

Thus, in what ways did Creative Partnerships offer professional development to teachers, what were the types of opportunity offered and what balance was struck between discrete CPD sessions and more embedded development work happening as part of working with students from day to day?

In their 2010 report 'Evaluation of the nature and impact of the Creative Partnerships Programme on the teaching workforce', Lamont, Jeffes and Lord developed a typology of the kinds of professional development work that was most prevalent within the Creative Partnerships programme. If we consider their findings we see there are particular sorts of staff development that are worth prioritising if a school is looking to inculcate a creative approach to teaching and learning. So what impacts did the Creative Partnerships programme have on a wide range of staff, including members of the school workforce who did not have qualified teacher status? What was the nature, range and extent of impacts and what evidence was there to support perceptions and claims of impact?

The NFER team developed a typology of impacts on teaching staff, based on their fieldwork and survey responses (from 2,295 individuals) that consisted of four 'domains':

- personal impacts (e.g. enhanced enthusiasm for job, own creative development, increased confidence, changed personal values, and developed personal learning);
- interpersonal and leadership impacts (e.g. improved skills for working with teaching colleagues, improved skills for working with creative professionals, and enhanced leadership skills);
- teaching and learning impacts (e.g. changed pedagogical values, use of increased/new creative language, new perceptions of pupils' learning, development of classroom practice, development of skills to help children's creativity, and curriculum development);
- career impacts (e.g. impacts on career pathway, new roles and responsibilities).

The most commonly-reported impacts on teachers were:

- development of skills for working with creative professionals
- enhanced confidence to try new things and to 'have a go'
- provision of skills to help children to be more creative
- enhanced enthusiasm for their job
- development of the curriculum in their Key Stage, department or school
- communication and sharing of their learning with other teaching colleagues
- development of skills for leading projects.

The most frequently-rated impacts from the survey results fell into the personal impacts domain, and the interpersonal and leadership impacts domain. Impacts from the career domain did not feature as highly, but a significant proportion of teachers still reported career-related impacts as a result of their involvement with Creative Partnerships.

A scale was constructed by NFER to quantify the overall mean impact reported by respondents. It showed that the average impact score is always highest for impacts in the interpersonal and leadership domain, regardless of the type of involvement with Creative Partnerships, amount and length of involvement, responsibility taken for Creative Partnerships and current career stage. This suggests that the kinds of changes in approach to pedagogy are enabling for teachers, providing a sense of autonomy and inspiring a sense of professionalism that boosts confidence.

There was a significant difference in the type of impacts experienced by teachers from the three types of Creative Partnership schools – Change Schools, Enquiry Schools and Schools of Creativity; teachers from Schools of Creativity were significantly more likely to report that they experienced impacts from their involvement with Creative Partnerships than teachers from other schools. Given the longer involvement many of these schools had with the programme and the intensity and duration of activities this is perhaps not surprising.

Those teachers who rated themselves as having 'considerable' involvement with Creative Partnerships experienced a significantly higher level of impact than those who rated themselves as having been less involved. Again, this suggests there is a lasting impact from engaging with creative approaches to teaching and learning that intensifies over time, rather than weakens. Teachers who had been working with Creative Partnerships for the longest time had higher impact ratings than those who had been involved for shorter periods of time.

There was a significant difference in the mean impact scores by level of responsibility for Creative Partnerships. Essentially, the more responsibility a teacher takes for creative teaching and learning, the higher the mean impact score in relation to impacts on their professional skills and confidence. And interestingly, there was no difference in the mean impact score for teachers at different stages of their career. Therefore, a teacher's current career stage did not seem to influence the nature or extent of impacts from involvement with Creative Partnerships.

Regardless of the factors applied, the biggest differences in average impact scores were consistently found in the career domain. This suggests that career-related impacts were most differentially affected according to length of involvement with Creative Partnerships, level of responsibility, amount of involvement and type of Creative Partnerships intervention. The factor leading to the biggest differences in mean impact scores was the amount of involvement in Creative Partnerships – in short, the amount of involvement (e.g. considerable, some or limited) exerts more influence over the extent of impacts than the other factors explored in the research.

The following case study narratives are reproduced with the permission of Creativity, Culture and Education (CCE) from Appendix C of the final report by NFER (Lamont et al., 2010). They give a flavour of how particular schools and types of teacher characterised the impact of the Creative Partnerships programme on their professional skills and outlook, and will be useful material to reflect on for a school beginning to develop a creative approach, particularly when planning a strategy for staff training.

Case study: A head teacher and a deputy head teacher and the shared impacts on leadership

The head teacher and the deputy head teacher of a primary school serving the needs of an ex-mining community in a deprived part of the UK were keen to raise the aspirations of their pupils. They became involved with Creative Partnerships in 2005 and have since worked with a range of creative practitioners including drama, learning and thinking practitioners, actors, poets and educational arts consultants. The two teachers worked together with Creative Partnerships from the beginning, and experienced shared impacts throughout.

Working with Creative Partnerships has had a transformative impact on the senior leaders' approach to leadership within the school

The senior leaders in the school (head and deputy head teacher, those members of the school staff who had explicit leadership roles or who were full-time class teachers but were part of the senior leadership/management team) are now more confident to plan and deliver activities in new ways, and are motivated to encourage staff to engage with creativity. They have learned to place their confidence in the effectiveness of creative practitioners, so they can advise and support staff in developing more creative approaches in the classroom.

The senior leaders' interpersonal and communication skills have developed across all levels

The teachers have become better at managing the expectations of different groups of staff within the school. They describe their work with creative professionals as a learning experience, saying, 'I now work with people from a completely different professional culture to my own'. The teachers have also learned to balance the needs of other staff within the school, including teachers, caretakers and office staff.

The senior leaders have now developed a creative curriculum across the school

The senior leaders now recognise the value of creativity across the curriculum, and recognise how their skills can make the curriculum creative. They are using this to plan a curriculum that will inspire children and motivate them to succeed.

The subject leader: changes in perceptions of pupils' learning

This subject leader has been a teacher for ten years, following a career in theatre and film. As a creative practitioner, his engagement with Creative Partnerships has been extensive. Having worked in a deprived urban school with mainly Muslim pupils on roll, Creative Partnerships has helped the subject leader to develop his understanding of pupils' preferred approaches to learning.

Working with a Muslim creative practitioner has helped the subject leader to understand the cultural background of his pupils

Prior to working with Creative Partnerships, the subject leader found it difficult to engage in creative tasks with pupils from a different cultural background to his own. He found that the pupils were often inhibited and, as such, it was difficult to foster creativity. Working with a Muslim creative practitioner helped him to understand more about the pupils' home life and the extent of their engagement with art and media. The creative practitioner has a very eclectic approach to creativity, which has encouraged more pupils to take an interest.

The subject leader now understands what pupils want to learn and how they feel about the school

Through understanding how his pupils engage with art and media, the subject leader has been able to find more effective ways to help them learn. The school has been involved in a 'Bollywood' Project, including external trips and experiential learning. It has been valuable for the subject leader to see work made specifically for South Asian audiences. This level of interaction with the pupils' culture has given him better insight into their perceptions of the school and a better understanding of how to engage them in creative learning.

The creative curriculum coordinator: renewed enthusiasm for teaching

Working with Creative Partnerships has transformed this creative curriculum co-ordinator's role within the school and her attitude towards her career. Prior to joining Creative Partnerships, the teacher had recently stepped down from her subject leader position, frustrated with teaching and no longer wanting the additional responsibility. Since becoming Creative Partnerships co-ordinator, she has renewed enthusiasm for her career and has responsibilities for whole-school change.

The teacher felt empowered by Creative Partnerships because she could tailor it to her school's needs and use it to make changes within the school

At the time the school began working with Creative Partnerships, the curriculum co-ordinator was very frustrated by her lack of autonomy as a teacher and felt that the staff were disheartened by a range of policy initiatives over which they had little control. Creative Partnerships changed her decision to leave the teaching profession because she felt more able to take risks and to be more proactive in planning the best for the children. She now considers herself to be a more proactive learner and is more interested in seeking out CPD as a result of Creative Partnerships.

The teacher now has the ability to teach in a way that makes sense for the pupils

In working with Creative Partnerships, the creative curriculum co-ordinator has had the opportunity to find innovative approaches to teaching that will benefit pupils. She is now more of a facilitator, taking more risks, and enabling more freedom and student-led learning. Her whole-school role has made her feel more enthusiastic and better equipped to take on new challenges within and outside of the school. Her more outward-facing role has also allowed her to seek out new perspectives and receive encouragement and advice: '...it's enabled me to be the teacher I want to be, not the teacher I was told I had to be'.

The advanced skills language teacher: Using Creative Partnerships as a tool to create new career opportunities

This teacher is an advanced skills language teacher (AST) with over ten years' experience of classroom teaching. Working within a large secondary school, she has been involved with Creative Partnerships for five years, and over this time has worked with a range of writers, producers, visual artists and architects. Creative Partnerships has given her the tools to bring about changes in her career pathway, and given her licence to develop her skills in new ways.

The case-study teacher has had experience of working with the senior leadership team

As an AST, she already has well-developed interpersonal and leadership skills. However, her involvement with Creative Partnerships has allowed her to exercise these skills in new ways to benefit her career. Within the case-study teacher's school, the role of Creative Partnerships co-ordinator is normally held by a member of the senior leadership team (SLT). Although the AST was not a member of SLT, she was the Creative Partnerships co-ordinator for nearly a year, which gave her a voice to drive forward changes and lead teams to devise new schemes of work. The AST plans to use this experience in preparing for a management position.

> The AST has used Creative Partnerships to devise new resources and a new curriculum, and has demonstrated to the SLT that creativity can be used to meet other priorities within the school
>
> The case-study teacher's temporary role as Creative Partnerships co-ordinator has given her access to the Senior Leadership Team and allowed her to make the types of decisions (e.g. regarding timetables, whole-school planning) that she would not normally be able to do. This has given her a sustained role and influence within the school and she has been able to introduce collaborative schemes of work with the support of the SLT.
>
> The NFER research highlights the overwhelmingly positive impacts for teachers of involvement with Creative Partnerships. High proportions of teachers consider themselves to have experienced a number of impacts, some of them very strongly, across the four impact domains previously listed. The robust nature of the study by Lamont Jeffes and Lord, drawing on responses from 2,295 members of the teaching workforce across a range of schools and types of Creative Partnerships programmes, reinforces the particular stories captured in the case-study descriptions above.

The impacts of Creative Partnerships on teachers and school staff

Most commonly, teachers reported impacts relating to their personal development, their interpersonal and leadership skills, or their own teaching and learning skills. Career-related impacts were less common, and emerged mostly for those with greater or more sustained involvement. Nonetheless, the findings demonstrate that the impacts of involvement with Creative Partnerships are far reaching and span a wide range. Involvement in Creative Partnerships does not, therefore, solely offer enhancements to teachers' own creative skills or use of creativity in the classroom, but it enhances leadership abilities, it impacts upon personal development, and for some, it leads to direct impacts on their career or development as a teacher.

Perhaps unsurprisingly, teachers who rate themselves as having engaged more fully with Creative Partnerships are those who reap the most benefit. Furthermore, those taking on co-ordination responsibilities, and those who have been involved with Creative Partnerships for some time, are also more likely to have higher than average impact scores. The beneficial influence of being engaged for some time with Creative Partnerships programmes reinforces the value of a sequenced and sustained approach to professional development.

Also noteworthy is that the main impact teachers experienced related to their individual professional development or career 'journey'. Hence, those involved largely judge Creative Partnerships to be a worthwhile form of development, perhaps not only because of particular skills and the benefits of partnership working with artists, but also because it offered a way back to a child-centred philosophy of education. When asked to compare Creative Partnerships to other forms of CPD, the majority of responding teachers felt that Creative Partnerships had a greater impact on their professional development; indeed only 10% felt that other initiatives and programmes had had more influence. This demonstrates the value placed on the Creative Partnerships programme by practicing teachers. When giving reasons for more favourable judgements, teachers noted that Creative Partnerships offered opportunities to develop and to use new skills, and as highlighted above, provided a sustained and whole-school form of professional development. The programme was also valued by teachers for the role it played in facilitating external relationships, and for the enjoyment that teachers took from it.

Creative Partnerships clearly offered a wide range of teachers in different roles and diverse schools positive opportunities to develop their skills and confidence with regard to creative teaching and learning. Transferring that potential to a school outside a national programme presents a new challenge, certainly, but not one that is insuperable. Where there were once local Creative Partnerships offices and many creative practitioners available to provide in-school workshops and sessions there is now, arguably, a more ad-hoc feel to local provision. But that need not prevent schools from designing staff training with creativity in mind. There may be self-organised networks of schools that can provide support and mentoring for the kinds of staff development creative learning inspires, and emergent groups of higher education providers can certainly give further back up and accreditation, for example, the Expansive Education Network (http://www.expansiveeducation.net), or Whole Education (http://www.wholeeducation.org), supported by the RSA. Such networks and alliances may well provide a supporting scaffold for a self-organised teacher development programme for those schools looking to begin or sustain a creative curriculum.

However, regardless of the ways in which such professional development may be sustained, there is a deeper question, which is the extent to which we are suggesting that teachers themselves become more like creative practitioners in their style and approach. Is this desirable or appropriate?

In some respects the answer to the above question must be 'yes'. The pupils in

Creative Partnerships schools, for the most part, based on all we can gather from the many research studies and programme monitoring reports CCE generated, clearly enjoyed the experiences provided by engaging in the process and through coming into contact with the creative practitioners. Children talked about them positively and often in terms of transformative effects on their self-confidence, their capacity to face challenges and on their relationships with other pupils and sometimes teachers. But as Galton (2009) points out:

> *to say this is to be accused of creating a 'them' and 'us' situation where creative practitioner equals good and teacher equals bad. Emily Pringle (2008) in her presentation to the Creative Partnership Seminar on Implementing Creative Learning, based on the findings from her doctoral thesis, makes a similar point.*
>
> *'In the contexts of CP consideration must be given to how and whether artist-led pedagogy can endanger broader and longer-term creative learning strategies across the school. One issue associated with artists' interventions in education (which these artists are aware of) is that art practitioners can adopt creative and experimental pedagogic modes because generally they are free from curriculum constraints whereas teachers are not always at liberty to do so. The artist thus becomes a creative 'other' whereas the teacher can be cast in the role of didact or policeman. There is a danger that artists reinforce normative relations because they act as one-off bubbles where they are perceived as limited outside interventions'. (p. 68)*

So what is to be developed here? Is it teacher's individual abilities to behave in ways more akin to creative practitioners? Or might it be more to develop the kinds of brokerage skills necessary to promote a greater degree of intervention in schools by successful creative practitioners? Should the focus not be so much on the individual teacher, but instead the culture of the school and the philosophy underpinning teaching across the whole organisation?

Whatever the 'right' way to implement a staff development programme in particular schools may be – and, of course, it will vary from school to school – it would seem that teachers adopting the practices of the more successful creative practitioners would be of value to pupils. Galton cites research from the US that was started in 1987 by the National Board of Professional Teacher Standards (NBPTS). The researchers sought to establish whether 'master teachers' – certified against a tight set of criteria as being advanced practitioners – did perform in their classrooms in more effective ways, thereby having a positive effect on student achievement. As Galton explains:

> *To gain master teacher status requires a rigorous examination costing a candidate US$2,000 and involves an estimated preparation time of several hundred hours. Candidates have to produce evidence of their pupils' academic performance together with portfolios and videotapes of classroom practice as well as undertaking a series of tests at an assessment center. The pass rate is low (between 10% and 20%). On the basis of the literature Bond et al. (2000) chose to specify expert classroom performance. Trained observers assessed these features by analyzing and numerically coding teachers' classroom lessons and video-taped transcripts. The comparison consisted of teachers who had succeeded and failed to gain the master teacher qualification. Observers worked 'blind' in that they were unaware of the result of each teacher's final assessment. (p. 70)*

The analysis by Bond illustrated that the following attributes, set out in table form in Galton's study of 2009, were found to differentiate the masters' from non-masters' classrooms. In the masters' teacher classroom:

1	Pupil exploration will usually precede formal presentation.
2	Pupils' questions and comments often determine the focus of classroom discourse.
3	There is a high proportion of pupil talk, much of it occurring between pupils. So that the metaphors 'teacher as a listener' and 'guide on the side' rather than as a 'sage on the stage' are characteristic of the lesson.
4	The lesson requires pupils to reflect critically on the procedures and the methods they used.
5	Whenever possible what is learned is related to the pupils' lives outside school
6	Pupils are encouraged to use a variety of means and media to communicate their ideas.
7	Content to be taught is organised around a limited set of powerful ideas
8	Teachers structure tasks in ways which limit the complexity involved.
9	Higher order thinking is developed within the context of the curriculum and not taught as a discrete set of skills within a separate course unit.
10	The classroom ethos encourages pupils to offer speculative answers to challenging questions without fearing failure

Table 5.1 List, Galton, 2009, p. 71

Reflecting back on the case studies and snapshots of practice set out so far in this book the above criteria do approximate to the kinds of pedagogy developed by creative practitioners working alongside teachers, suggesting that some of the features of good quality creative teaching are modelled by creative practitioners in ways that form a basis for ongoing professional development.

6 Creative Artists and Their Practice – Do They Really Add Value?

Creative Partnerships was predicated on the hypothesis that there is something unique to artists and other creative people that can help unlock or increase creativity in young people and teachers. Do they bring additional value to teaching and learning or can creative approaches develop just as effectively in schools without them in the long term? This chapter discusses where the line between good teaching and artists' skills and competencies might be drawn and why sometimes it may be important to have both involved in particular projects.

Creative practitioners whose daily work is driven by practices not determined directly by schools and curricula bring a different perspective to learning and they approach and solve problems differently to others. Creative Partnerships was always interested in understanding what, if anything, was different or unique about creative workers and what happened when such people acted in partnership with teachers. Of course, teachers themselves are naturally very creative people, but the distinction here is between those whose practices are somewhat determined by the way the education system itself is structured, with its various rules and staging posts, exams and assessments, and those whose habitual styles of work are determined by other structures (indeed sometimes a lack of formal 'structure') and ways of thinking.

In 2006, CCE began a process of researching these creative characteristics, firstly through studies by Galton (2006) and McLellan et al. (2012) and, as Creative Partnerships began to wind down as a government-funded programme in 2011, a study by Thomson et al. (2012) looked at what were described as 'Signature Pedagogies', those particular patterns of work, and differences in use of available resources that point to some sort of unique 'additionality' offered by artists and other creative partners. This chapter will focus on the learning from these studies and consider in what ways the principles might be made use of by any school.

To begin with I will set out a descriptive case study from Thomson et al. (2012, pp. 33–35) of an interaction between artist and children. This contains within it, I suggest, salient features that we can return to when we reflect on what may or may not be 'different' about an artist working with children as opposed to a teacher.

Case Study: Signature Pedagogies

Iona, Environmental Artist

This Creative Partnerships Allotment Project took place during the summer term of 2011 with a Year 6 (aged 10 and 11) class in an inner-city primary school in the Midlands of England. The relatively new, low-rise, school building sits beneath a tower block of flats in an area of the city formerly known for textile manufacturing. Disused factory buildings are a prominent feature of the local landscape. The project was led by a single creative practitioner named Iona, an artist well-known for her work elsewhere in the same school and with other schools in the locality, but new to the particular class. This was a one-off project that took place through three separate meetings: the first in the classroom, the second in the hall of the local Quaker Meeting House and the third on the artist's allotment. The artist also returned to the school to support the teacher while the class were engaged in creative work reflecting on the allotment visit. The project was not, however, primarily related to producing art works: the focus was on creativity and well-being more generally, in a period when trips out felt more manageable after the stresses of tests that had taken place earlier in the month and before the children moved on to secondary school.

The first session was based round a PowerPoint presentation that Iona had put together from her personal photographs, the first of which showed her dressed as a 'flower fairy' pushing a litter cart. The focus of Iona's talk was her personal experience, interests and beliefs and the art works and performances she had devised. She encouraged the children to identify with her emotions and guess what she was thinking when the photographs were taken. As the session progressed, the themes running through Iona's talk emerged more clearly. The flower fairy concept neatly introduced a recurrent focus on the natural world and also served to signify Iona's interest in trans-formation through peaceful protest, creative arts and community action. The pace of these exchanges was brisk but unhurried. Iona's tone was friendly, matter-of-fact and inclusive. ('I can't wait for you to come and see my allotment! I'm going to let it be a surprise to you when you come, but [putting up a photo of a pear tree] look at these pears!') She addressed the children in a generally adult-to-adult manner, dropping in personal details and listening carefully to any points the children cared to make. She conveyed both deep seriousness about her work and the sense of joy and fulfilment she derives from it.

Iona made no attempt to shield the children from the painful side of life, though the framing was always positive, personal and art related. She used examples of problems, setbacks and false starts from her personal history to illustrate the importance of her message about perseverance and self-belief.

The other over-arching message of this first session was about everyday creativity: that, with effort and imagination, something could be made from virtually nothing – 'you can use something that you would throw away and make it permanent'. These were to be the themes for Iona's next two sessions with the class.

Before the class visit to the allotment, there was a session focussed on self-expression through the arts. This pre-figured the allotment visit in several important ways. It happened off site in The Friends' Meeting House, a community space that was unfamiliar to the children. As before, the resources for the session were idiosyncratic and provided by Iona but, as with the allotment session, the main teaching method was the facilitation of independent activity. The focus was on producing representations of stress, and then of contentment, through the production of collages. The materials for making the collages were stored in what Iona referred to as her 'Tinker's Box'. The Tinker's Box comprised about 30 small crates full of beads, the hooked lids of shower gel containers, cones, feathers, drinking straws and other, mainly plastic objects derived from domestic or packaging sources. The children assembled – and later dismantled – the collages on large circles or squares of coloured card. They worked individually in a self-chosen space on the hall floor, having selected their own collection of materials from the Tinker's Box. Once they were satisfied with their collage, they were encouraged to write about it, in prose or in poetry.

The patterns of Iona's language use were similar in many ways to those of the first session, but the focus of this second meeting was on the children's experiences and creativity, so she offered no anecdotes or sustained personal references. The emphasis of the session was on exploring, creating images, interpreting symbols, finding language that captured emotions. Instructions were couched gently, as invitations. Most of Iona's time in the session was spent crouching on the floor in private conversation with individual children, listening to their points about their work. This was in contrast to the teacher, who was also circulating and showing obvious appreciation for the art work, but offering semi-public suggestions and prompting certain interpretations. Photography was used as part of the recognition of each child's efforts ('Can I take a picture of that?' The child nods and smiles and they both look at the photographed image together). The use of photographs also served to develop the theme – introduced in the first session – of making something from nothing and, in doing so, creating something that persists. The session was designed to appeal to different senses and to offer multiple modes of expression. The focus was on the self, rather than on Iona as an artist and personality. This paved the way for the third session, the allotment visit, which Iona had planned as a multi-sensory experience to be explored multi-modally.

The allotment is a triple plot, surrounded by high hedges, near the top of a hill and overlooking the predominantly working-class area of the city where Iona lives. Grassy lanes run between the hedges demarcating the plots, and entry to Iona's allotment is through a privet arch and a high wooden gate. Three buildings sit on the plot. The 'huckleberry shed', a cooking area with a camping stove, shelf units and a brightly decorated awning, abuts on to a 'reflection room', a wooden shed with sofas and soft furnishings. Between the two, a curtained area offers some privacy to the rudimentary toilet facilities. Near the top of the plot, at the crown of the hill, sits 'The Sky Palace', a large dark blue structure made of reclaimed glass windows and doors with a lean-to on one end. The allotment is loosely divided into areas. There is a large raised bed, a picnic table with benches, a hammock under some trees, a wild brambly stretch along the back end, a flat grass and dirt sitting space and a fire pit. The whole plot is decorated with found, reclaimed objects: a bath tub pond, a pillar of car tyres decorated with CDs, pitted metal advertising shop signs, a wash basin on its side, shoes with plants growing in them, plastic barrels. A wooden ladder set against the huckleberry shed gives access to its gently pitched roof, which is partially covered with bedspreads. Tools – wheelbarrows, forks and trowels – and containers of varying sorts are arranged around the plot.

One child, coming up the lane and through the gate into the allotment, commented that it was like being on the TV programme *I'm A Celebrity, Get Me Out of Here,* a reference that captured some of the strangeness of the environment for the children. Iona, who had been waiting for her visitors, welcomed them to 'my land'. She took enormous pride in the allotment and assumed that they would be bowled over by what they saw.

Most of the session's activities were conceptualised as 'jobs'. They included: cutting up vegetables to make soup over the fire for lunch; sorting bulbs that had been retrieved from a public park; barrowing bricks from the bottom of the hill; transplanting marigold seedlings; painting a plastic barrel; winding in the hose pipe; decorating bird-scarers made from CDs. There were also leisure and craft activities: modelling with clay on the picnic table; playing darts in the Sky Palace; music making with the xylophone and a ringing bowl on the roof of the huckleberry shed; sleeping or swinging in the hammock; taking photos and video with the school's cameras. And there were other allotment holders to meet: Jack, 'the Elder', who kept chickens, and Robbo, Iona's friend, who had a pigeon loft on his plot.

Iona modelled how she did the jobs and the leisure activities. She showed the children how she sat on the shed roof, watching the sun rise and making her bowl ring. She told them how she'd been feeling ill the previous weekend, so had sat in The Sky Palace, resting and thinking. She mentioned that her nieces were planning a sleepover in the Palace. She showed them how to tend the fire, chop the vegetables, prepare the barrel for painting with masking tape, distinguish between hyacinth, daffodil and tulip bulbs, and handle the seedlings gently. The children responded warmly to what was being offered. In the open discussion sessions they elicited from Robbo that he spent about seven hours a day on the allotment, that Iona's family spent time there helping her and relaxing and they probed the relationship between the plot and Iona's art. At the close of the session, the children asked some very practical questions which suggest their different experiences of the artist's and the teacher's pedagogies. They asked their teacher:

Boy: Are we going to write a recount of this?
Girl (before the teacher could respond): A diary, probably.

The questions to Iona were:

Boy: Can I come again?
Iona: That would be lovely. But you're in Year 6 now.

> Girl: I'll visit school every time they come on a trip here [i.e. return from secondary school]
>
> Girl: Who will take over the allotment?
> Iona: I don't know. I've no plans to leave.
> Boy: Can I? Can I take over the allotment?

There are several striking features of this brief case study and Thomson et al. elaborate on them at greater length than I am able to here (2012, p. 36–38), but to single out just one aspect, there is a clear invitation into the artist's world, into the realm of their emotions and motivations and to an immersive experience which is about an alternative way of living, based on an activating certain preferences, particular sorts of choices. The children's experiences are qualitatively different as a result and the kind of learning they are engaged in goes beyond the transmission of facts and knowledge. Instead, they are guided to a deeper understanding:

> *The class were explicitly encouraged to be interested in Iona's personal 'obsessions' and to appreciate the things that she loved. Within the initial classroom based group experience, there was both metaphorical and physical space to be yourself. The children sat in their normal places in a darkened room with their chairs turned towards the whiteboard. They were free to guess, interpret and comment, to make their own links, if they wished to. There was no pressure to contribute and no sense in which a point could be deemed wrong or irrelevant. The PowerPoint images and commentary were unpredictable and the session meandered, but it was obviously going somewhere: not to a single, pre-determined goal, but towards the development of individual understandings of what might make someone want to live the kind of life that was being described. The major resource in the lesson was the artist herself and her willingness to lay herself open to scrutiny.*
>
> (Thomson et al., 2010, p. 36)

While it is difficult for teachers to re-create this kind of open and very personal invitation on an ongoing basis, there is a broader point to reflect on about the extent to which teachers feel able to engage emotionally with the children they teach, and the degree to which they can be open about their own trials and errors when it comes to teaching and learning. While the reality that all pedagogy is inexact and constantly changing, or in some cases, however depressing this may be to admit, is replaced with 'drilling' for tests which children seem increasingly aware of and deflated by, there rarely seems to be any space for this to be openly dealt with as an issue. In the account above, the rather deflated reference about 'doing a recount' of the allotment experience, through to other examples we'll come on to later in this chapter, there is often an undercurrent of children seeing through unspoken rules of an 'education game' and that the artists working on projects, with a completely different set of reference points and rules, are able to supplant with an experience that feels much more authentic.

Pedagogic practices of creative practitioners

Reflecting on Creative Partnerships practice generally, and taking account of the wide variety of practice and project objectives, this authenticity of experience is one of the chief unifying themes running through successful Creative Partnerships work. Thomson et al. postulate a set of pedagogies that, while not exclusive to, are particularly well developed in artists. When taken together they may form a repertoire of practices that model elements of creative learning. These are set out below, reproduced from Thomson et al.'s final report, and they imply what some of the key additional benefits of creative practitioners in school settings may be.

Repertoire of pedagogic practices

1 **Provocation.** A provocation is an object, image, sound, person, event or action that is deliberately ambiguous, unexpected, strange, out of place, open and contingent. It does not arrive with a predetermined interpretation. It is intended to act as a stimulus to meaning making, a trigger for individual and collectives to draw on their own knowledge and experiences in order to provide a meaningful response to what is on offer. It provides a platform for thinking of ideas and possibilities. What the provocation wants from participants is that they give it narrative substance, an explanation, a rationale, a legitimate place in their location.

2 **Use of artefacts.** We noted a preference for the use of found, rather than commercially-produced objects; the treasuring, display and curation of everyday objects imbued with great personal or cultural significance; the creation of new, special, everyday resources. Photographs functioned both as a record and reminder of the work and as artefacts in their own right, recognising and reifying otherwise transitory experiences and creations.

3 **Moving out of the classroom.** The artists were much more likely to move beyond traditional classrooms. They used studio spaces, but the work often moved into available spaces in the local community. The artists recognised the

---

importance of particular local places and found different ways of populating the spaces. The Delius theatre group, for example, ended their play in a choreographed sequence that garlanded a disused building in bunting and surrounded it by actors in movement. To rehearse this scene, students were bussed across the city, from south to north of the river to an unknown and somewhat 'enchanted' space (an early nineteenth-century gin mill, now part of a film studio complex) near the Olympic site in east London.

4   **Making an occasion.** Performances and exhibitions are central to the processes, but the readiness to create special events, celebrate and appreciate was a feature of most of the teaching we observed. The vision was often large-scale and involved the whole school, for example at Spencer, Delius, Larwood and Rowan schools, where Mike worked. The dance project at Badger Wood was ambitious. St Hilda's was prepared to 'think big' in organising the whole-school engagement in its 'Creative Olympics'. The performance in which Delius students were involved took over the entire outdoor space of a three storey Victorian school. Combined with the commitment to the quotidian and the local and the readiness to work at scale, creating occasions helped make the ordinary special and validated the creativity in everyday life.

5   **Use of 'the texts of our lives'.** There was a continued and appreciative interest in the following: community stories and funds of knowledge; porous borders between school and home knowledges; a readiness to translate and re-imagine events, stories, characters in familiar settings (in the work of the story teller and story-makers, for example, but also in Iona's and Stanley's work). This validated and included students and their families in ways not generally found in mainstream curriculum approaches

6   **The self as a teaching resource.** The artists tended to speak openly about their personal lives; they assumed that students were interested in their identities as artists and they shared information about their own experiences. Some self-consciously presented themselves as role models (Tunde, for example). Because of the difference in their role, the artists seemed more open and less defensive in this respect than most teachers. They were less risk averse, more inclined to touch students and less concerned about school rules and safety regulations. This contributed to the sense that things were more free and open in artist-led sessions.

7   **Costume.** The artists tended to dress less formally than the teachers did; the costume requirements for their roles in school were different to the expectations about teachers' clothing. This had some symbolic impact on the teaching context. Specialist clothing was an important aspect of some dance and drama work, and dressing up in character costumes signified expanded or new teaching roles. Marianna, the 'Story Lady', for example, wore a costume which had been carefully constructed to be an exaggerated, almost comic book representation of a storyteller. When working as Story Lady, Marianna was in

character, but she did not wear the costume or call herself Story Lady when she was working with the children to conduct interviews, construct stories or develop and rehearse the performance. In this way, Marianna demonstrated to the children the difference between front and back stage work, using costume to enable her to move between roles (for instance, to discuss the stories as texts to be interpreted responsibly).

8 **Use of the body.** There was more movement, greater use of the body to make meaning, more attention to the development of physical skills, gesture, mime – and a greater sense of the need to co-ordinate with other people's bodies in shared endeavours. This was particularly obvious in the dance and drama projects: at Delius, the theatre company Sober Senses exhorted students to 'explore' what the body can do to communicate meaning; and physical involvement was also, for example, a feature of Jim's and Mark's story-making and Tunde's storytelling.

9 **Different classroom discourse patterns.** The patterns of classroom talk differed from traditional teacher/student exchanges. The tone and style of the talk differed from conventional teacher-talk in that it was often highly personal and anecdotal. Unlike teachers, the artists did not explicitly identify the learning objectives they had in mind for the group. There were clear, often moral, messages in their talk, but they were delivered more as warnings or beliefs than as lessons. The underpinning logic of the artists' talk was not generally the school logic of cause and effect (hard work bringing reward; misdemeanours bringing punishment); it tended to be a looser logic of going with the flow, trying hard and trusting that things will probably turn out right if you approach them cheerfully and with good intentions. The most marked distinctions between teacher and artist talk related to the work the students were engaged in producing: teachers were more oriented towards judging quality and artists were more concerned about the inherent meanings of the piece.

   Some of the artists spoke to students at considerable length. Iona for example showed the class 106 slides in her first session (and the children enjoyed listening to her). The artists asked and answered fewer questions than teachers. They used a lot of analogies, but explained less than teachers typically do. They tended to avoid giving feedback, other than in situations where praise could be offered. They encouraged guessing and welcomed suggestions, other than in the strongly professionally-framed sessions.

10 **The creation of a rich narrative environment.** The artists' own uses of analogy, anecdote and personal history, combined with a freeing up of the classroom atmosphere, a widely shared interest in local and community stories, and a readiness to improvise and use drama tools, supported the creation of rich narrative environments in many of the classrooms.

11 **The use of professional norms.** One theatre company observed the research team working at Delius School, ran workshops, initially within drama lessons,

around some of the main affordances of physical theatre – awareness of space, of precision of timing, and of ensemble work: 'we're exploring what the body can do'. The discourse and the practice of ensemble were the main elements of dramatic 'discipline' that the company introduced to the classroom, and along with these came an emphasis on the transformation they required in the behaviour of students: 'We're a company now. You're NO LONGER students'. The point was elaborated to stress, again, the specific, distinctive qualities of performance: 'this is what we do it rehearsal...this is physical theatre'. There was no sense of negotiation in these utterances.

This insistence on establishing professional 'not school' norms was also very clear in the Badger Grove dance project, and observable in the Blair College media project. The professionals' general talk with the students was informal and focussed on the inter-personal, but a large proportion of the exchanges were concerned with solving the practical problems and challenges of the work at hand. This highlighted the expertise of the professionals, which was also evident in the ways they made judgments and applied standards from their field. Sometimes these judgments and standards were made explicit, at other times they were not. Quite often, the students had to strain to comprehend the implicit and the tacit. At Badger Grove this desire seemed to be deliberately built into the project: initiating and behaving like the professional was how much of the learning seemed to take place.

In these professionally-oriented projects, the students were made aware that the everyday practices were specific to the area they were working in. The models of teaching and learning contrasted with models on offer in their schools. Students frequently made reference to the specialness of these situations; despite the absence of teacher-facilitated reflection on the differences, the students developed their own comparative framing of the pedagogic differences.

12 **Alignment with disciplinary expectations.** At Spencer Comprehensive, the framing of the creative arts practice was very strongly through the discipline of Fine Art. Students worked autonomously, alongside their teachers and the artist in residence. The language was about self-expression, form, technical and aesthetic problems. Some aspects of the pedagogy were analogous to the professionally-framed sessions: the focus on individual skill development, for example, and on spending the time necessary to get the task done properly, rather than fitting the tasks to the allotted time. The 'rules of the game' were laid down through modelling, the organisation of space and – more explicitly than in the case of the professional norms – through direct instruction in the lower years of the school. Within this disciplinary framing, and in contrast with the professionally-oriented sessions, the traditions of Fine Art were a frequent point of reference as the students learned about and looked at work from different periods and different artistic movements. The study of art and the development

of aesthetic responses were central to the identity of the school, and through the school's practices they were made available to individual students as part of their own identities. At Delius, though without specific reference to traditions of theatre and performance art, aspects of the discipline were clear, notably encouragement of awareness of space, and of the movements and being of other performers within it.

13 **The valorisation of collective endeavour.** Because of the predominating attitude towards inclusion, plus the fact that the teaching was generally intended to bring people together into a shared endeavour, the emphasis was on sociality. Whole class teaching and direct instruction were commonplace. The emphasis was on involvement, collective creation and sharing rather than on individuation and competition ('we're a company now, you're no longer students – Delius). Even where the work was individualised, as at Spencer, the collective endeavour was to construct a studio environment where art practice flourished. There was a weaker sense of the hierarchy of achievement than there is in many other lessons and a stronger sense of collective accomplishment.

14 **Managing behaviour differently.** Creative practitioners tended to rely on students' commitment to the collective endeavour, the professional or disciplinary norms, the virtuosity of the artist's display of expertise, the use of praise and careful listening. Because the artists were actively seeking not to individuate or exclude, and because their frames of reference did not tend to include school rules interpreted at the classroom level, their behaviour management techniques were different to teachers'. Generally, they worked extremely successfully and students seemed to feel both respected and respectful. Occasionally, the artists had to call upon the teachers' expertise in behaviour management if the norms they had established were disrupted.

15 **The use of routine.** The artists used routines to create atmosphere and a way of being in the class, to reinforce norms of their discipline (rehearsal, warm-up, etc) and to produce the group performing as one responsive voice and one networked body. Their routines were distinctively different to everyday classroom routines (for example, the routine of getting changed in the Badger Grove dance group, which was based on professional norms).

16 **Flexibility in pacing.** Characteristically, the teaching we observed was brisk in terms of pace while feeling unhurried. This is in marked contrast to lessons where pace is explicitly related to a sense of urgency about time running out. In England, the orthodoxy of 'good lessons' (e.g. for inspection purposes) is that they are segmented, with 'starters' and plenaries and smoothly-managed transitions between activities that encourage students to be attentive and do not allow them time to get bored. The underpinning metaphors here are economic – spending and investing time wisely to maximise its efficient use.

In the artists' sessions, events took time; time did not tend to dictate the event. In contrast to lessons where tasks might be cut short by the bell, or teachers create obvious time-filling activities because they have misjudged how long a task will take, the artists demonstrated a very strong commitment to the work that was being created – the dance, the artwork, the story, etc. This in turn led the students to invest more seriously in the work. This was an important element of the modelling the artists provided (an example of which would be the children who explained to Iona how she had inspired them through her commitment to her artwork). On the whole, **rhythm** and **flow** were highlighted rather than speed.

17 **The use of open-ended challenge.** In contrast to lessons with pre-specified learning outcomes, the matter of what exactly would be learned in the artists' sessions tended to be quite open. The trajectory of the lesson was not so much about following a road map as journeying together and seeing where the group arrived (the dance, story-making and allotment projects had this quality in common). At the start of the creative practitioners' sessions, the challenge was often presented as being just out of reach but probably attainable through collective hard work. This gave sessions a feel that was distinctly different to lessons where the learning outcomes are chosen and asserted by the teacher in advance. The artists' sessions celebrated challenges met through hard work, in contrast to lessons where failure to achieve the required learning becomes the main marker of distinction.

Also, it was observable across all of the sessions that the practitioners were at pains to stress to the students that there was no definitive right or wrong answer to artistic problems. The emphasis was on whether the work looked and/or felt right to the student in the context of what else was happening in the class. So standards were apparent and applied, but individuals were expected to develop their own skills of discrimination and judgement. There was therefore a stronger orientation towards intrinsic rather than extrinsic motivation and evaluation in the artists' sessions.

18 **Building commitment to the community.** As well as building sociality within the group, the artists were all very positively oriented towards the schools' wider communities. Their artistic practices were about the remarkable nature of everyday life, rather than the exotic or esoteric. For each of them, the notion of creativity itself offered a 'way in' to new connections with the community, bringing the worlds of school and home into closer contact with one another. The performances and occasions created new opportunities for parents and member of the wider community to build new and different connections with the school.

This philosophy, combined with the collectivist approach they adopted and the emphasis on the agency and creativity of each individual, sometimes resulted in a 'campaigning' edge to their teaching. Whilst the political dimensions of topics did not tend to be explored, the artists talked about their beliefs and the impact of their work and in doing so suggested alternative modes of dissent and critique.

19 **Permission to play.** Several of the artists used silliness, eccentricity and 'larger

> than life-ness' to gently disrupt taken for granted ways of school thinking and doing. Silliness sometimes had obvious links to direct and school-sanctioned learning: for example, Mike encouraged the children to 'speak like bees' starting every word with 'zzz', which not only took concentration but was also absurdly amusing to everyone involved. This was part of his continual word play, his appreciation of children's sense of humour; he taught the children a new word each session that they then needed to use appropriately throughout – 'loquacious', for example, became incorporated into handkerchief characterisation and plot development.
>
> (Thomson et al., 2012, p. 39–45)

Benefits of creative practitioners to creative learning

In an earlier study, by Galton (2006) there are a number of findings that reinforce the notion of there being particular additional benefits to be gained from partnering with creative professionals. In this study 11 creative practitioners were selected from six schools (three secondary and three primary) in three Creative Partnerships areas around England. There were three dancers, two environmentalists, one filmmaker, one photographer, one musician, one drama director, one visual artist and one conceptual artist. All worked for a minimum of six weeks in the school and the pupils chosen were from classes with no previous extended exposure to Creative Partnerships. In this way it was possible to establish base line measures of attitude and motivation prior to the intervention.

Motivation was an important concept for the study. In the same way that Thomson et al. (2012) found an extended definition of value amongst creative practitioner's work that stretched well beyond practicing for tests and learning facts, so Galton noted a clear distinction between pupil motivation in order 'to reach the required National Curriculum level' and what we might call learning for learning's sake. In fact, there is evidence to suggest that the better many young people become at doing the bare minimum to reach required levels in tests, the worse they do in terms of high quality learning behaviours – the ability to undertake challenging tasks independently, to take pleasure in finding things out and to be resilient in coming back to tasks that at first seem difficult and require multiple attempts to solve or achieve. As Galton puts it:

The pupil's behaviour when faced with a challenging task is not only a function of the personality, expressed in terms of basic drives, but is also influenced by the manner in which pupils cope with failure. If a pupil attributes failure to a lack of ability he or she may react entirely differently from a peer who believes the result will be largely determined by the amount of effort required (Weiner 1992). Dweck (1986) who argues that the view the child takes about ability is crucial to motivation, has taken these ideas a step further. If ability is thought of as something fixed then the likelihood is that pupils holding this view will feel that they can do little to alter the course of events when faced with a task that they believe is too difficult for them. Only pupils with a strong belief in their own competence will be highly motivated. Others with little confidence in their innate ability are likely to display a response known as 'learned helplessness'. In contrast pupils who accept that through increased effort previous failures can be overcome will concentrate on mastery of the task rather than concern for where they stand in relation to their peers (Dweck and Leggett 1998).

(Galton, 2006, p. 9)

This resonates strongly with the allotment case study featuring Iona, and the notion of choices based on beliefs determining outcomes. Essentially, Iona was presenting herself to the children and helping them to understand how she came to be the kind of person she had chosen to become. Galton finds a similar trait in artists, particularly when they are first meeting pupils.

When creative practitioners first meet with pupils there seems to be several immediate goals which they seek to achieve. The first of these concerns is the kind of relationships that they are seeking to establish. In every case they begin by giving a potted version of their life history. What distinguishes it from what a new teacher might say to a class s/he hasn't met before, of the form 'I'm Mr Smith and I'll be taking you for History,' is that the creative practitioners' accounts are often accompanied by expressions of feeling about certain past events which are offered as explanations for certain choices. Thus Alex at Ashby Grange with a Year 4 class and Pam at Merryweather with Year 5 tell the pupils:

> *I'm Alex and I'm a dance artist and I live in Portsmouth. I've worked with lots of junior groups and parents and tots. I've been a dance artist*

> *on Creative Partnerships for two years and it's made me realise this is the work I like doing; it's the kind of work I enjoy doing most.*
>
> *Hello I'm Pam. I write and direct plays and I also act. I didn't train in drama. I did a degree in modern languages which led me into teaching but fairly quickly I became a teacher of English and drama because that was where my heart was...I then became a writer working with young people on drama and loved that too so now I combine work in the professional theatre with work for Creative Partnerships in schools.*

At Woodstock, Glynn arrives late for the first morning and tells a group of pupils, a mixture of Years 8 and 10:

> *My name's Glynn and I'm a filmmaker. I'm sorry I'm late; blame the trains, but it's made me anxious because I wasn't here to set up before you came. I've been doing this kind of work for some years now and I got into it by helping out with groups of pupils who were excluded from school – so I had to learn the hard way.*

Whereas an introduction such as 'I'm Mr Smith' etc. seems designed to establish the respective roles of the participants and, to a certain extent, reinforce the power relationship between the teacher and the class, those of the creative practitioners appear to take the form of an opening conversation gambit which signifies a more equal relationship. In Glynn's case there may also be a secondary purpose, in that his task at Woodstock is to work with groups of disaffected pupils, and by telling them about working in a referral unit he indicates he has seen and can cope with most manifestations of disengagement.

(Galton, 2006, p. 34)

So creative practitioners, in Galton's study, seem to represent in ways similar to those described in Thomson et al.'s later work, an alternative set of approaches and values that can be thought of as different to 'the norm' in school and beneficial in specific ways. In particular, Galton noted there was a premium placed on risk-taking. By this, he refers to relatively low-level, every day risk – the unknowns and 'what ifs' that give room for learners to move into and colonise as their own, as opposed to the style of teaching where the already known answer is artificially kept hidden and is slowly revealed by a much more directed pedagogy. This has echoes of Creative Partnerships own planning and evaluation processes, as outlined in Chapter 2.

Scaffolding, familiar to teachers through the work of Vygotsky and others, is one way of managing risk taking. Through this process activities are created which provide the right balance of support and stretch in order to keep pushing pupils beyond their comfort zones but without undue pressure. Creative practitioners also use several other strategies. Artists seem to appreciate that many of the reasons driving the pupils' responses are emotional rather than cerebral. Teachers, on the other hand rarely attributed pupil behaviour to feelings.

Galton (2009) cites a recent study by Ravet (2007) which looked at teachers' and parents' explanations of pupil disengagement:

> *Most of the teachers' explanations involved deficit theories (either of attitude, ability or personality) or attributed disengagement to contexts outside the control of the school (home situation, family background or peer relationships). Parents, on the other hand tended to attribute lack of interest in school to feelings of boredom, shyness or fatigue. (p. 50)*

Creative practitioners tend to work in a way that may be advantageous if the reasons for pupil disengagement are to do with boredom, lack of real 'stretch' in activities and a fear of failing to make a particular grade. They operate precisely at the emotional level where fear of failure often determines pupils' response to challenge. One way this is manifest, Galton suggests, is for creative practitioners to reveal their own feelings in a natural, almost casual way 'as if conveying a message to the pupils that talk of this kind is acceptable currency among the group' (p. 51). This relates strongly to the findings of Thomson et al., where, during encounters with pupils, creative practitioners often included emotional statements about who they were and why they chose to do what they do. Galton notes how often creative practitioner use emotions to explain the reasons for their decision making.

> *In one instance, for example, (the creative practitioner) Bridget is faced with a persistent request from a keen student to add snow to the trees that have been constructed and painted as part of the scenery for the pantomime, 'Snow White and the Seven Dwarfs.' This girl wants to add bits of paper, painted white to represent snowflakes.*

> *Bridget: I like your suggestion but it's been a hard afternoon with everything that's being going on. I'm a bit stressed and can't cope with any new ideas at the moment. So can we leave it for now? I'm not saying it isn't a good idea. It is but not now. OK?*

Compare this to an episode when pupils at another school are editing their photographs.

> *Simon [to class]: Are you happy with that? We need a title.*
> *Teacher: Stained glass snake?*
> *Pupil: What about stained snake?*
> *Teacher: Sshh! We've chosen.*

(Galton, 2009, p. 52)

In summary, for Galton, when compared to teachers in Creative Partnerships schools, creative practitioners:

- Gave pupils more time to think when planning and designing activities.
- Extended questioning sequences so that classroom discourse was *dialogic* rather than consisting of the more usual *cued elicitations*.
- Offered more precise feedback.
- Tended to extend rather than change pupils' initial ideas.
- Built appropriate scaffolding into the task instead of using teacher-dominated approaches such as *guided discovery*. The former while lowering risk of failure maintained the task's ambiguity while the latter often reduced the pupils' uncertainty about what was required to a point where there was little likelihood of arriving at an unacceptable answer. Task related scaffolds appeared to encourage pupil independence whilst teacher directed ones spawned increasing dependency.
- Were more consistent in their management of learning and behaviour.

They were more likely to offer explanations when refusing pupils' requests and in dealing with negative behaviour they frequently referred to similar incidents in their own past, thereby indicating to the pupil that while they were unable to condone certain actions they understood the reasons why such incidents occurred.

As I have already emphasised previously, there is no attempt here to suggest that somehow these attributes and characteristics are the preserve of the creative practitioners alone, and that they are never present in teachers' repertoires. However, it is suggested that, on balance, the attributes highlighted through the examples in this chapter tend to dominate for creative practitioners while they tend to be sublimated for teachers – possibly through the demands of a test-focused curriculum and the plethora of very public pressures that relate to that, from school league tables to Ofsted inspections and grades. Where the creative practitioners are rooted in philosophies and practices that do not have to relate strongly to or be bound by curriculum pressures, they do, ironically, have much in common with what we might broadly describe as a high-quality, child-centred, intrinsically-motivated forms of pedagogy. A culture of learning for its own sake, rather than learning to perform for tests.

7 Creativity in Schools and Parental Involvement

This chapter will discuss the pivotal role parents have to play in children's learning and the ways in which creative projects can offer opportunities to engage parents, particularly those who have disconnected from school or for whom school has never been a strong focal point. Creative Partnerships was always interested in parents as key stakeholders and many projects sought to gain their involvement and participation. The idea underpinning this was that it would be a shift in a broader culture of family learning, where parents were as interested as their children, which would offer the best chance of sustained improvements in schooling, particularly with an accent on the kind of creative learning the programme was most interested in. This chapter briefly summarises the responses parents had to Creative Partnerships, their views about the projects and the effects they had on their children and relates their new vantage points to the important notion of parents as key drivers of the 'appetite for education'. After setting out parental views about creative education and how that helped re-ignite creativity in schools, the chapter will reflect on what the implications for schools and teachers may be.

Parental influence on children's learning

Many studies have shown the variety of ways in which parents directly affect the education process. One of the most influential was Jerome Bruner's *Process of Education* (1960). It placed an emphasis on the influence of parents on children's 'predisposition to learn', all those formative experiences that help steer the individual to a mindset where learning is enjoyed for its own sake and where there is a sense of curiosity and questioning is highly developed. Bruner suggested that, of all the influences on a child's ability and desire to learn, schooling itself was only a minor factor in establishing such predispositions. He also suggested that education is about more than the curriculum, standards or testing, reminding us that it encompasses the child's broader social, cultural and emotional learning too (Bruner 1996). More recent work – Desforges and Abouchaar's (2003) review of research into the effects of parental influence – concludes that developing a child's positive self-concept as a learner is largely defined by parent-child involvement. Like Bruner, they note that schools are, in a sense, relegated to the position of serving a pre-established interest in learning rather than firing that interest up for the first time. Quite whether or not the role of the school is so sharply demarcated as these studies suggest is not clear, the overarching point of the importance of parents or carers in first establishing and then sustaining good learning habits, is irrefutable.

Creative Partnerships was a programme that certainly sought to engage parents whenever the possibility arose and this tacit belief in the involvement of parents and the longer term benefits of family learning was a defining factor in many successful projects. In order to understand this aspect of the programme better we commissioned the Centre for Literacy in Primary Education (CLPE) to undertake research that could more clearly describe what was going on. Anecdotally, those of us managing the Creative Partnerships programme often came across casual descriptions of parental involvement and our hunch was that something significant might be taking place. The research aimed to test this hunch and give us a deeper sense of the mechanisms that might be causing a better quality of engagement with parents.

The CLPE has a long-standing interest and expertise in creative forms of education and has invested a great deal of research time in describing the affordances of these approaches and the possible benefits they bring to teaching and learning. The CCE-commissioned study (Safford and O'Sullivan, 2008) builds on prior work from CLPE – *Animating Literacy* (Ellis and Safford, 2005) and *Many Routes to Meaning* (Safford and Barrs, 2005) – which began to probe how parents relate to the opportunities of Creative Partnerships in schools.

The research was based on a mixture of questionnaires and in-depth follow up interviews. In the summer term of 2006, a questionnaire, which had been trialled previously with a smaller number of schools, was sent to senior staff in 200 Creative Partnerships schools. From this survey, 65 questionnaires were returned. From the returned school questionnaires, follow-up interviews with 16 senior school staff and with 34 parents in 13 schools took place in the academic year 2006–2007. The study aimed to explore the following questions:

- What do parents themselves think of creativity initiatives in schools? How does a creative curriculum reach parents in ways that the 'core' or 'basic skills' curriculum does not?
- What activities or approaches engage parents in the school and in their

children's learning? Are there models or approaches that are more effective than others?

- How are creative partnership experiences, activities and projects made available to parents and in what ways? How are creative partnerships and new learning opportunities for children explained and offered to parents?
- What is the impact and effectiveness of such experiences, activities and projects on parents' attitudes, expectations towards and about children's learning? Are there are patterns of exclusion and participation amongst parents in these contexts?
- Do parents feel that creative partnerships contribute to a distinctive school ethos or learning ethos? Do creative partnerships contribute to parental satisfaction with the school? Do creative partnerships impact on the wider school community?

Children talking about school in the home – why is this important to parents?

As previously noted, Desforges and Abouchaar (2003) point to important links between parental involvement and pupil's learning behaviours. They also draw attention to the fact that those children who invite parents to engage with their schoolwork are motivated more by the enjoyment they get being in the company of their parents than in a belief that it will improve their performance academically. We were interested to find out whether and how creative approaches to learning may be creating openings for children to invite their parents to talk to them in this way.

Safford and O'Sullivan (2008), after looking through evidence from Creative Partnerships schools, argue that children's interest and enthusiasm about creative projects provides new contexts for parents to communicate with children at home and with the school itself. In the interview data, parents relay how their children begin to talk much more about schoolwork, sometimes 'incessantly' about creative work, which is in stark contrast to the norm, where they would tend to not say much about school at all. Through this new enthusiasm to communicate about developments in class, parents feel more informed about school generally. For example:

> Usually you ask them and they're doing 'nothing!' at school. They actually come home and tell you – and they can't wait to tell you, rather than you having to ask them.
>
> (Pauline, Safford and O'Sullivan, 2008, p. 36)

I've got to say, my eyes and ears were wide open because I couldn't believe what he was telling me [about the film animation work he was doing].

(Phil, ibid)

They talk openly about what they've been doing. They're more confident at speaking. You don't have to drag it out of them. Everything's coming out of them…children tell parents and then parents feel they'd better come in and have a look.

(Joe, ibid)

Parents repeatedly conveyed the feeling that creative projects helped children become more enthusiastic about participating in school and also brought about improvements in children's attitudes towards the whole-school environment. It became a place they wanted to be, and where they did things that became important to talk about.

I used to hear about the filmmaking every day – you [usually] never hear anything about school. It was less about that final event, the experience they had of developing their ideas and shooting the film brought them far more than a single event…it's brought a greater enthusiasm for school which has a knock-on effect on everything they learn at school. …[my son says] 'I can't wait to get in on Friday because we're filming this scene' – I think that's got to have a positive effect on everything else that goes on that Friday to be honest.

(Steve, Safford and O'Sullivan, 2008, p. 39)

The important point of shared enjoyment is key in these moments of talk between children and parents. Parents were usually very impressed with the skills children learn in creative projects and the processes they go through. Talking about what has to happen to undertake a project using filmmaking equipment, animation, sculpture, dance, singing, interviewing, or gardening reveals how inclusive the work can be. Every child has a voice and can participate and this comes through strongly in the testimony from parents:

My son in Year 6 is severely dyslexic. Now he knows he can express himself through construction, through artwork. The projects gave him confidence. He knows now that he has particular learning styles. He has been able to build up his awareness and confidence through creative projects. I know that we would have had real behaviour problems on our hands otherwise... Creative Partnerships should promote itself to parents. Parents want this. I made an appeal to a secondary school to get my son in there next year – based on its Creative Partnerships funding, continuity and philosophy.

(Kerry, Safford and O'Sullivan, 2008, p. 40)

Learning shouldn't be just about sitting them at desks and the teacher talking at them, and them writing notes and answering questions. Learning comes through play, through art, through watching other people, through doing things at home and at school. We all have different learning styles, don't we? We can't say what works for one child will work for the next.

(Pauline, ibid.)

What do they get out of it? Enjoyment! I wouldn't want them to go to a school where it was purely reading and writing and getting answers out of them. I want them to have a wider scope for what they think about and what they enjoy, and I want them to enjoy school and life beyond school. I know they'll learn to read at the end of the day. But I do want them to have a really wide, rich experience of life....If I knew a secondary school was a Creative Partnerships school I would think about sending them there – it would be a factor in my consideration.

(Catherine, ibid.)

These perceptions suggest that parents view creative programmes as making a positive difference to their children and therefore want to show enthusiasm for their children's developing skills and talents in order to keep that positive outlook towards education developing over the longer term. This can lead to parents reinforcing children's interests beyond the school, usually through family outings or additional clubs or classes during school holidays, after school or weekends. This shared 'capital', the kinds of emotional investment made together as a family, can be a crucial factor in longer-term educational success for young people.

How creativity helps shift parents' views on children's learning and the role of the curriculum

The discussions prompted by creative work at home can lead parents to feel they understand a great deal more about their children as learners. Moments of surprise at children's developing interests and the high quality of their work are often precisely the moment a deeper interest begins to develop. Parents begin to see children learning in wider contexts, and parents who have had more traditional experiences of education often revise long held opinions of how children learn and where and how learning can take place.

> *It has definitely changed my view about what learning is about for children. It's fun! I look at them when they are doing these things and they are learning so much, and they've enjoyed their day. And every time I go into town now I have to stop at the bookshop for art books.*
>
> (Tanya, Safford and O'Sullivan, p. 48)

> *For my son, it was the project 'How Things Are Made': how bridges stand up, structural things. Now, if ever we go down Trent Bridge, we have to pull over: 'Let's have a look at this bridge and how it's made!' It's sparked my interest. I can see it's made and see it's there, but I had ignored it. Now, I want to know how it's made and how it stays up there. Wonderful questions no parent can answer! We went to Lincoln Cathedral which I thought might be too formal, too boring. My son loved it, the fact of the architecture, the windows with the light coming through. We all loved it – his dad, his sister. It was a place that normally we would have drove past. But we thought, we'll stay and have a look. Now when we walk through town, it's looking at the buildings and the windows and everything – then coming home and building it with Connex! It was all from that project.*
>
> (Nicole, ibid)

Parents who participated in the Safford and O'Sullivan study felt Creative Partnerships played a significant role in boosting children's confidence, self-esteem and pride and took the view that these benefits were linked to children being able to freely express themselves in such projects. What expressing oneself means in the context of Creative Partnerships is directly linked to the kinds of creative skills and behaviours the programme attempted to inculcate – the chance to try things out, the confidence to try things again if they fail first time round, the authenticity found in working on projects that have been based on your own ideas, and made possible through your own efforts, skills and tenacity. Parents seemed to relate strongly to this, realising that for many of their children it had offered insight into an alternative way of setting out educational experiences that make learning engaging.

> *You can't do it wrong, can you? You interpret something or make it your own. [My daughter's] confidence bowled me over. My husband sometimes says some of the things they get involved in are too grown up – but he went to [the performance] and ate his words. I cried! It was lovely. It was so professional, to get up on a real stage and do it for everybody. There were 200 to 300 people there.*
>
> (Geraldine, Safford and O'Sullivan, p. 50)

Parent's views on the long-term benefits of creative learning

In the CLPE research, parents noted that they had observed the positive impact of school-based creative work on their children in areas beyond the specific skills of the project. They suggested that children's creative work appears to boost confidence, gives them the desire to try new experiences and to test out the 'unfamiliar'. Parents also pointed out that they saw this effect continuing as primary school children transferred to secondary school. And perhaps most significantly, parents felt their children's participation in creative projects broadened their sense of possibility and offered a window onto alternative jobs and ways of working.

> *It opens things up for them, things they might not think of doing. It builds up. When they move on to secondary school they can go on to build on it. Once they get given a chance, they realise they can build on it and move on.*
> (Orla, Safford and O'Sullivan, 2008, p. 35).

> *It gives them an outlook on ambition. My daughter will come home and say 'I want to be an actress, a fashion designer' – it's always something on the creative side rather than a mundane office job and I think that's really good. I know that when I was in primary school I didn't have any idea of what I wanted to do when I grew up, so talking about a career and a creative career is just fantastic.*
> (Louise, Safford and O'Sullivan, 2008, p. 42)

These perspectives show a clear awareness that creativity offers children the kinds of 'knowledge, flexibility, personal responsibility and problem-solving skills' which may help them to adjust to shifting and challenging future employment prospects (Banaji et al., 2006, p. 56).

Parents also expressed a sense that Creative Partnerships projects instil valuable qualities in children such as application and self-discipline.

> *My son for nine months now hasn't spent a single penny of his pocket money because he's saving up for this £600 camera. It's going to take another two years! But now he won't spend a penny because he wants a proper camera – and that is purely from this project. I am pretty impressed with the discipline of it…My oldest son didn't have these opportunities and he struggles with hobbies and what he wants to do. My younger son used to be quite shy – a meek child really – not putting himself forward – and now he's not just behind the camera he's out in front, and he's become a performer which he never was before in the slightest! His whole personality has grown, and it's hard to get that from school, I think.*
>
> (Steve, Safford and O'Sullivan, 2008, p. 47)

This notion of creative projects offering a foothold to young people onto real-life opportunities, rather than acting as a sort of therapeutic counterbalance to the core curriculum is noteworthy, the implication being that parents come to feel that the 'core' curriculum is less 'real' and meaningful to their children than one focused more on creative learning. If they feel that children are developing skills and knowledge that offers access to wider life experience beyond school it is a point to reflect on for schools whose remit, in the broadest sense, is always about more than just exams and tests and also encompasses the development of rounded, confident, engaged individuals who have a sense of autonomy about their future, embracing both the opportunities and challenges it will bring with equal relish.

Parents as learners

Finally, there is an important finding from the research project by CLPE that relates to parents themselves and their attitudes towards their own learning. Many of the parents interviewed left compulsory education at the earliest opportunity and memories of their own school experiences were often negative, sometimes even distressing. This was particularly so when their own recollections were set against the very different experiences their own children were having as a result of participating in the Creative Partnerships initiative.

> *When I was in school, everyone played the guitar. But I couldn't play the guitar, so I was stuck playing the tambourine in the corner. And I hated it. There was no other choice. I was humiliated. With things now, there are so many new instruments from cultures around the world, everyone can have a go and not feel inadequate. I feel it's really important for every child, regardless of their ability, to have a go at something and feel equal to the child next to them as much as possible. With these creative projects, everyone wants to have a go.*
>
> (Chrissie, Safford and O'Sullivan, 2008, p.33)

> *I went to school in the dark ages. We never had anything like this. We were made to stand on chairs if you did something wrong. It was OK to completely humiliate children.*
>
> (Stephanie, Safford and O'Sullivan, 2008, p. 34)

> *You daren't breathe when I was in school. Parents didn't get involved. My mother would never have had a syllabus from me, she wouldn't have had a clue about what I was doing in school.*
>
> (Sandra, ibid.)

Promotion of parental involvement in school life and children's learning, the idea that schools are welcoming places of spirited partnership and looking to work with parents actively is still a relatively new concept, as can be seen from the rather bleak picture painted by the quotes above. Is it any surprise that many parents still feel unsure of how they should fulfil such a role, and many schools can struggle to get very far beyond newsletters and 'homework contracts'? The interview data from the CLPE study strongly suggests there is a need for schools to set out 'low risk' invitations for parents to become involved in aspects of school life. This implies a sensitivity toward the possible negative predispositions parents may have about school and about learning. Parents were very clear about their sense of uncertainty about engaging with schools:

> *Philip: A lot of parents work don't they? But a lot of it I think is a fear – a fear that they'll have to get involved, and commit. Not maybe so much*

commit – but they've seen the standard of homework that their children get from this school and some can't do it, and basically they don't want to make themselves look stupid cos they don't understand what their child's doing. They put maths and English courses on for the parents, you get a qualification out of it.
CLPE: Is that enjoyable?
Phillip: No.

(Safford and O'Sullivan, 2008, p. 35)

A lot of children come to school and are bombarded with English, maths and science. Then they go home. Mum and Dad work. The TV is a babysitter. A lot of children may not be creative at home, or do baking or crafts. I know a lot of parents would like to – but life doesn't always give you the time.

(Stephanie, Safford and O'Sullivan, 2008, p. 36)

Parents joining the creative learning journey

These responses by parents are directly relevant to teachers' concerns about improving children's educational experiences and their academic achievement. The raft of evidence available pointing to parental interest and engagement in education as being a key precursor to a child's chances of success presents educators with a clear call to action. It is important to see parental engagement as a vital ingredient in a child's educational success and it is incumbent on schools to employ strategies that will succeed in getting parents on board. It was the case with Creative Partnerships that parents were often inspired to re-engage with their own children's learning by reconnecting with their own self-development. There were many examples of parents doing something for themselves as a result of a Creative Partnerships project. This included such activities as visiting museums or other cultural venues, taking up classes of some kind, often related to creative practice, or pursuing new hobbies or new employment. Some of the mothers that took part in the CLPE study went on to become full or part time teaching assistants or lunchtime play supervisors as a direct influence of having been involved in a creative project. The CLPE noted how for many women, who may have been out of the job market while raising a family, creative programmes offer some important first steps to jobs or training.

I run a craft and card-making club. That was something that came from school. Now I supply three shops. And I've got three boys in my club, learning different techniques of card-making.

(Jeanette, Safford and O'Sullivan, 2008, p. 38)

Having been out of the workplace for five years, it brings your confidence back. I was 'just' a mum, now I'm back to being a person. The first time I had to stand up in assembly because of the parents' group that we run, I was so nervous. Even my daughter said – 'you was scared Mummy weren't you?' But the last time I did she said – 'You was better that time Mummy!'

(Tanya, ibid.)

Their learning becomes your journey as well...You start to remember things and you think – I know how to do that, I can do that!

(Asa, ibid)

There were also examples of parents finding a new appetite for cultural pursuits, choosing to visit places of interest and venues that are connected in some way to Creative Partnerships projects. This is sometimes simply because children want a repeat visit to somewhere they visited as part of a project, or it may be because a new understanding develops about such venues and what they can offer because the artist working in the school makes families aware of opportunities.

We went to Doncaster, the museums in Hull, the Earth Centre. It was a brilliant place, we had a fantastic day, and the children adored it. We couldn't believe it when they closed it.

(Sandra, Safford and O'Sullivan, 2008, p. 39)

Connecting schools and communities

We have seen the extent to which parents believe that creative projects made children feel better about themselves and more positive about their schoolwork. It is interesting that in articulating the benefits of this work they also touch on the fact that it is still only partially available. Through Creative Partnerships there was some level of co-ordination and coverage across all English regions, but by no means was every school included. Parents showed a desire that these opportunities should continue and be made widely available. They understand the value of recursive opportunities for children, and are concerned that the current cuts in funding could further limit the reach of this kind of work.

> *It was really good to go somewhere and perform. I felt quite excited about that for the kids. They were on stage. People were listening. That was really good. I had never been there [the cultural centre] before. It was an opportunity for me as well. I had seen pictures on the telly, but it was my first time there. Now, I see pictures on the telly and I say – I've been there!*
>
> (Gayle, Safford and O'Sullivan, 2008, p. 42)

> *They get a feeling of being part of the community. Like the mosaic, it's always going to be there. For our girls, it was their last year and it was leaving their mark on the school. They know it's still there. Even now, in secondary school, they still come and play in this playground because there aren't any other places to play around here. It would be nice to do more work that is lasting.*
>
> (Brenda, ibid.)

In some cases, parents feel that creative projects lead to all-around better communication from the school, and they express appreciation for projects that 'break down' walls between school and community through exhibitions, performances or parades which take the school out into the community.

Community performances and exhibitions enable parents to see their children's schoolwork in a heightened, professional context. Creative programmes that involve children in activities beyond the school (performing, exhibiting, visiting) help parents to see children's learning within a community and sometimes a professional context, and encourage some families to become involved in cultural activities outside the school. These out-of-school locations are important in engaging parents who may be reluctant to enter the school itself.

Summary: The benefits of creative learning for parents and how schools can embed this in their practice

The creative curriculum has a positive impact on home-school communication

Children's talk about creative projects at home offers parents a way in to schools. As interest and enthusiasm grows through these moments of sharing news and relating the twists and turns of an exciting project, parents become motivated to find out more and often get more directly involved in children's learning and in the wider life of the school.

What can schools do to make this happen more often?
In a sense, of all the benefits the parents talked about, this one is the most organic, in as much as the children's enthusiasm is natural and authentic and flows freely from the projects themselves. It is probably worthwhile for schools to make parents aware of any shift towards a creativity-focused curriculum, so that the stories related by children can be understood in a particular context of curriculum development.

Home discussions

These home discussions help parents to develop new vantage points about their children as learners, and give them an insight into the kind of supportive role they might take on themselves.

This sense of 'efficacy' (Hoover-Dempsey and Sandler, 1997) is a very significant benefit. As parents get inside the experiences their children are having through their talk and ongoing enthusiasm it affords parents the chance to situate themselves within the experience and give themselves an active role to play. This leads to them joining in with children's interests in a range of ways, as Safford and O'Sullivan suggest: 'either by contributing their own skills and expertise, by learning alongside children, or by ensuring children continue these interests in after-school clubs or classes' (p. 47).

What can schools do to make this happen more of the time?
Schools are great nodal points in the community, offering so many different sorts of opportunities to children and their families. When creative projects are happening in school, it is worth considering making available information that might be considered an invitation to take a 'next step' – the kinds of cultural visits, clubs,

activities that families might be able to do together and also be developing a shared enthusiasm for. As one head teacher who spoke with the CLPE put it:

> We took the children to the art gallery and they came back absolutely buzzing about it. Then you can send home publicity about all the art gallery has to offer in terms of family workshops, and all of a sudden parents begin to think, 'Yes, that's something we could do' (Safford and O'Sullivan, 2007). It's starting with the children and using that to raise parents' awareness of what the locality has to offer...It's not just 'come and watch your child perform', but more about the process, getting parents to sit in and see what we're doing.

Motivation

Parents suggest that creative projects increase motivation for children to be in school and have a role to play in overall development and life chances of each child.

Safford and O'Sullivan cite Hoover-Dempsey and Sandler's key construct of parents as being their personal and defined sense of their own children's uniqueness; this individuality and the sense of 'becoming' rather than 'being' seemed to link well with a creative curriculum that provided real opportunities for discovery, risk-taking, collaboration and questioning. This blend of aspects being personalised by each child's type and level of engagement, giving them a chance to get a greater feel for who they are now and what they might want to do in the future. It also provided a window onto alternative ambitions through real links to professionals in a range of less well-known jobs, or portfolio workers who do more than one form of work linked by an underlying principle or aim.

What can schools do to make this happen more often?

The key element here is the presence of creative professionals within the school, alongside teachers. Although the government-funded element of Creative Partnerships is over, there are still many ways schools can bring external creative professionals into the school to model different ways of working in partnership with teachers. Linking the work of visiting creative professionals to stated school priorities, to a School Improvement Plan or similar long term planning document, gives projects a rootedness and authenticity that stops them being seen merely as 'relief' from other forms of learning. Bringing artists, architects, scientists, gardeners, storytellers, poets, dancers, musicians, actors, writers – the list goes on – into the school can model other kinds of work for children and provides pathways to self-discovery that many young people would otherwise not explore. For schools in England, Creativity, Culture and Education,[6] the Arts Council England[7] and the recently announced 'Bridge' organisations it funds,[8] can all offer advice and guidance as to how a school might effectively commission work by external creative professionals and artists.

Creative Curriculum

Parents believe that a creative curriculum can contribute strongly to a distinctive school ethos where children and parents feel pride in their school. We have seen from the chapter focused on ethos earlier in this book, the particular ways Creative Partnerships shaped the overall atmosphere and personal ethics within a school. Often, a school develops a very distinct identity through creative projects, partly made visible through artworks and inventive uses of space, but also in a recast set of relationships between staff and learners. Parents suggest their children's sense of connection to schools that have such an ethos can continue even after they have moved on, particularly where projects generate a lasting legacy in some physical form –architecture, murals, mosaics, sculptures or redesigned gardens.

How can schools help to make this happen more often?

The development of this creative ethos is detailed more in Chapter 3, but in all its forms, a school that is strongly influenced by creativity, to the extent that it's overall sense of purpose and styles of working are transformed, begins with an acknowledgment of the different viewpoints, approaches to work and processes of thinking and interacting that many artists and other creative people bring with them to projects. We will detail some of these particular 'habits of mind' in the next chapter. Often, that difference is the key to a shift in ethos – new ways of questioning, alternative approaches to failure, ways of collaborating in a deep way, taking joint ownership of project and ensuring there is potential to learn within a project for all involved. Schools interested in building such an ethos might expect to explicitly address the following: a shared definition and vision of creative learning; a structured approach to planning as a means of making all participants' expectations clear to themselves and each other; a developed sense of knowing what to look for, new skills to value, and particular ways to inculcate them; and a shared process for review and future planning whereby creative projects are built into the long-term cycles of planning for the school.

A range of models of creative partnership can successfully involve and engage parents

The fact that creative projects were taking place in schools made connecting with parents much easier. The projects create a shared interest between school and parents – the common 'talking point' that begins with children taking home narratives of their experiences. At the most basic level, the connection is made and parents come to see final products and attend performances. While this is a good thing, the most successful Creative Partnerships projects went further. A deeper engagement sustains family involvement beyond the life of an individual project and increases the chances of a positive, successful time at school for learners. Getting buy-in from parents to a more sustained relationship with school, keeping that sense of interest and engagement 'live' requires a good deal of effort, but with the importance of parental involvement almost beyond question in terms of a child's educational success, such effort is certainly vital and worthwhile.

How can schools help to make this happen more often?

To take parental involvement beyond attendance at shows and performances, schools could consider the following: inviting parents to participate in earlier stages of planning and development with creative professionals; they might make use of interactive displays; they could implement a more varied set of meetings; and they could try adult versions of children's creative experiences. In the CLPE research, it was noted that those schools which utilised Family Link workers and offered Family Learning support through courses and training sessions as part of a creative curriculum were able to engage parents more deeply and retain their participation after the life of the project. Also, as was noted by Safford and O'Sullivan (2008, p. 53), greater cross referencing between strategies for Family Learning and creative programmes would almost certainly increase the potential for growth in volume and quality of parental involvement in the life of the school.

A creative curriculum can offer low-risk invitations to parents to become involved in school

One of the most interesting and practical findings from the CLPE project was revealing the importance of 'low-risk' invitations for parents. Safford and O'Sullivan suggest that parents perceive creative projects as an invitation while they see the core curriculum more as a demand. Given that many parents, particularly within the kinds of areas of deprivation Creative Partnerships operated, may have mixed experiences of school and in some cases they have rather negative memories, a creative curriculum therefore has the potential to reach parents more readily than core curriculum projects which can often reinforce a sense of personal inadequacy about particular subjects – maths and English, for example. A well-established, ongoing creative agenda can provide a wide range of invitations and opportunities to parents which are more likely to be perceived as welcoming, non-threatening and proactive. These invitations have the power to make a positive difference in parents' involvement; they send clear messages that parents are welcome and valued by the school.

How can schools help to make this happen more of the time?

Low-risk invitations are those which remove the barriers to engagement and lower the stakes around what has to happen after the invitation has been accepted. So, in the case of creative projects, especially as we know children talk about these projects at home, giving parents the chance to comment on the work they will have heard about is a good option. This might be either through writing a comment, as they might in a homework record, but in the spirit more of offering an emotional response or celebrating the achievement. Or it might be through visiting the school to see a piece of art, a new learning space, not necessarily to use it or participate but initially just to see it and be able to comment on it: it creates a reason to share the positive feelings children express at home, to echo those sentiments where appropriate, and thereby opens a new channel of communication when other creative projects take place in the future.

Another option is to offer practical opportunities for parents to do creative things as part of an adult group. In interview, senior school staff related to the CLPE researchers that they were 'more than willing' to come into school 'for things that aren't going to threaten them if they can't read or write properly' (ibid, p. 49). Some examples of how schools have offered parents 'low-risk invitations' are included in the report by Safford and O'Sullivan and are reproduced here:

> *They enjoy the practical things: gardening, massage and jewellery courses. We had a make-up course and a dozen parents came, Christmas crafts, keeping fit, line dancing – anything we can think of! We're trying to show that just because you had a bad experience [in school] it's not going to be bad now. You're not going to be asked to do anything that you can't do.*
>
> (MH, head teacher)

Quite a lot of parents have a barrier about coming into school. They don't feel very confident in their own literacy/numeracy skills or feel that for them school wasn't a very positive time. They feel it's too daunting to come in and be part of something. If we're doing arts projects we get a higher level of response because it's less threatening. Less would come in for a literacy or numeracy project. There were 40 parents [for a storytelling session] which was unheard of. We never get that kind of response.

(SJ, head teacher)

Parents often lack confidence in their own ability to contribute to their child's learning. Once we can get them here they usually enjoy it and comment positively. Sometimes it is difficult to explain what a creative project entails specifically and they are wary of getting involved.

(PH, co-ordinator PH)

A creative curriculum can reconnect parents with their own learning

Creative Partnerships activities in schools showed that parents can use creative projects as a means of reflection, a way of understanding their own experience as learners. Often, this can lead to parents connecting with new learning opportunities for themselves, as well as remaining engaged with their children's education. Creative approaches to learning reach beyond the school to directly engage parents and communities. A key learning point from the CLPE research was how the sense of being valued by the school in creative projects emerged as a factor for parents, and a perception that the project takes them to a different vantage point where they feel more connected to school. We know from the DfES (2003) that parents want more and deeper involvement in schools; a creative agenda is an effective way to work towards higher levels of participation.

How can schools help to make this happen more often?

Evidence suggests that a creative curriculum, combined with low-risk invitations will re-engage parents with their own children's learning. We have also heard how it can lead to parents reconnecting with an impulse to learn for themselves, to take up a new skill, or continue with some form of creative practice that a school-based project gave them a chance to try out. Schools can play an important role in encouraging and signposting parents interested in pursuing their learning journey. In the UK several Local Authorities have offered a number of Family Learning opportunities where parents and children can take classes in digital filmmaking, drawing and painting, photography, drama, storytelling and song-writing. Whilst some of these classes take place in schools, all of them take place outside of school hours, effectively extending the school into the community. The extent to which such provision can endure during times of funding cuts remains to be seen, but if schools are aware of these follow-on opportunities they are in a position to act as a signpost for parents looking to learn more. For example, Lambeth Education Authority in London did much valuable early work to effect the integration of the creative arts and Family Learning programmes, principally through work with the Royal Festival Hall, the Hayward Gallery and a number of other arts organisations and practitioners in the South Bank area. Lambeth have found that this approach appeals strongly to those hard-to-reach parents who had been disconnected from their children's schooling experiences. There are likely to be local equivalents of these organisations, large or small, with a vision that encompasses 'family' engagement and learning. Schools that are aware of what is on offer and that see it as part of their role to offer advice and direction would be invaluable to parents.

Signposting and knowing where it is possible to go to take that 'next step' is certainly a key part of extending the interest of parents. In the next chapter we turn our attention to how identifying and planning the next steps is still at the heart of the challenge we face when it comes to engaging young people in the classroom. What does progression look like for young people developing their creativity, and is it possible to assess this in a way that offers a more nuanced way forward when planning for learner development?

8 Creative Assessment and Progression

While Creative Partnerships was able to point to strong evidence of impact in terms of attainment in traditional subject areas, such as literacy, where agreed methods of assessment and criteria for levelling students is in operation, it was a fresh challenge to be able to show how children had become more creative. Anecdotally, there was a great deal of testimony and narrative suggesting that people were developing their creativity as part of the programme, but CCE was keen to explore whether it was possible to assess progress in ways that might constitute a system or framework, something that would be used in many schools in broadly similar ways and serve as a legacy for the programme. In this chapter, we will explore the possibility of such an approach to assessing learning, and describe the ways Creative Partnerships tried to surmise how creativity itself was being enhanced for individuals involved in the programme.

It is probably useful at this point to recall other forms of assessment and monitoring that were used as part of the programme, and to consider the tool we are about to discuss in proper context. At the beginning of this book, we mentioned the Creative School Development Framework (CSDF), the high level assessment of where a school as an organisation identifies itself in terms of its own creative development (see Appendix 3). We also had, at a level below that, an evaluation framework that questioned and reflected on the efficacy of the projects as they happened in schools and an early iteration of this framework is set out in Chapter 2 (it subsequently evolved in form and content, but is recognisably rooted in that first approach). All participants were able to give their view, and were asked to reflect on elements of creativity as part of that process; the objective being to think of the successes or weaknesses of the project as a creative experience as well as a vehicle for enhancing other areas of subject knowledge, often from the core curriculum. What neither the CSDF nor the project evaluations did was offer a framework for closely observing or a means of tracking the development of creative attributes in *individual learners*. In order to do that we would need to either use an existing measure of creativity if it was deemed suitable, such as the Torrance Test, or devise a new one that seemed to us fit for purpose.

Assessing creativity – what are the choices?

As a way of figuring out whether an existing measure or combination of measures might work as a way of meeting this challenge, we commissioned a study by the Centre for Real-World Learning (CRL), which is based at the University of Winchester (Spencer, Lucas and Claxton, 2012a). Much of this chapter will draw on work from that study, and to begin with will reference the literature review that was undertaken as part of their project. The CRL team's remit was to assess the main debates and methods for assessing creativity in individuals, to consider whether they might be pressed into use as a way of evaluating impact within Creative Partnerships, but more importantly, as a potentially longer term framework teachers could use to plan for progression in creativity so that as pupils moved through their school careers there would be a sense of discernment, some element of control and a degree of purpose to the kinds of creative opportunities offered. In short, a way of assessing creative learning that would allow the kinds of skills it comprises to be developed in targeted ways.

A survey of the literature on creative skills and attributes illustrates that it has become relatively common to find aspects of creativity being assessed, but only rarely within schools. It is much more likely to occur as an aspect of workforce development in other areas of working life. Psychometric tests are often utilised as a means of comparing individuals vis-à-vis what are often referred to as 'soft skills', a catch-all term that will often encompass skills that might be associated with creative behaviours. According to Sefton-Green (Sefton-Green, J. 2008), while it is the case that there are significant differences between 'soft skills' and creativity, there is also a degree of overlap between them. He suggests that such skills and behaviours are 'part and parcel of what it means to be a creative person' (p. 21), and often play an instrumental role in success within the work place – for example, the abilities to collaborate, show empathy towards peers, problem solve or come up with original ideas.

In their helpful literature review looking at progression in creativity, Spencer, Lucas and Claxton (2012b) set out a summary of the diverse range of tools that have been developed to assess creativity in disciplines such as engineering and social psychology. These comprise a raft of different instruments and metrics including 'ratings scales; interviews; checklists; peer, parent, or teacher rating; observations;

assessment of end products; personality tests; biographical sketches; aptitude and ability tests; problem finding and solving' (p. 47). The review also points to the many cognitive based online tests available that allow some insight and profiling about elements including the degree of openness to creativity,[9] the ability to think creatively,[10] and the degree of right- or left-brain dominance.[11]

Citing Plucker and Makel (2010) the literature review by Spencer et al. lays out a number of categories into which the main assessment tools for creativity can be organised and understood:

- Psychometric tests for *divergent thinking*
- Behaviour or personality tests of *past behaviour* or *personality characteristics*
- Personality tests of *personality correlates of creative behaviour*
- Activity checklists of *experience associated with creative production*
- Scales assessing *attitudes towards important aspects of creativity or divergent thinking*
- Advanced techniques for the assessment of *creative products*
- Expert judges to assess *level of creativity in a product or response* (Consensual Assessment Technique)
- Six components to assess *creative design of product* (Consumer Product Design Models): newness, ability to resolve problems, level of pleasure induced, ability to match needs of customer, importance to needs of customer, level of desirability or criticalness

Plucker and Makel add a category, suggested by Amabile and colleagues (Amabile et al., 1996), that argues for an instrument to assess the *climate for creativity* within particular contexts. In ways that echo Creative Partnership's own Creative School Development Framework, this 'self-report' instrument throws light on the viewpoints of individuals in relation to their working context – the factors in the background that may set the conditions through which creative work can thrive.

By and large the approach most often adopted to gain some measurement of creative abilities and development of creative skills is psychometric in nature. Spencer et al. (2012a), again citing Plucker and Makel, argue that the plethora of psychometric style tests may have less to do with its suitability as an approach to creativity as a concept and more to with:

> pre-existing interest its developers had in other cognitive phenomena. Having studied factors associated with variance in such phenomena as

> *ability, aptitude, and intelligence using similar methods, natural cross-ferti-*
> *lisation led to psychometric approaches (such as tests for divergent thinking)*
> *being used to measure creativity.*
>
> (p. 48)

One of the best-known tests of creative thinking, the Torrance Test, provides an example of a school based psychometric approach. The test uses divergent thinking as a proxy for creativity. E. P. Torrance explained the rationale for this as follows:

> *Children are so accustomed to the one correct or best answer that they may*
> *be reluctant to think of other possibilities or to build up a pool of ideas to*
> *be evaluated later.*
>
> (Torrance, 1970)

The test aims evaluate divergent thinking and some other problem-solving skills. These skills are scored in relation to the individual's degree of fluency, originality, and elaboration where those generating the most ideas win higher scores for fluency; originality of ideas corresponds to the extent to which the ideas are unusual from the norm, and where flexibility relates to the multiplicity of categories of response; finally, elaboration is taken to be the individual's ability to use an initial idea as stimulus and then self-generate new variants and themes without further prompts.

Despite this comprehensive sounding suite of tools, tests that probe divergent thinking, such as Torrance, are not without their critics. Some critics point to the fact that test conditions, particularly the way the test is mediated (whether individuals are timed; whether they are given specific instructions; whether the test is treated as a 'test' or a 'game') greatly affect the outcomes in terms of originality and/or fluency scores. So the scientific nature of the test and its links to pseudo-scientific 'hard' outcomes in terms of a summative 'score' or quotient is affected by social factors. Also the test itself, like many tests, can be practised for and 'learned' without the respondent necessarily cultivating the skills being assessed in their day-to-day behaviours, or their styles of learning. These questions and possible inconsistencies can deter many researchers and educators from opting for psychometric tests of this type. It is also difficult to see how such tests, requiring as they do, training both in terms of administration and analysis, could provide teachers in classrooms with a useful tool, practical and with a professional validity they can recognise in relation to their own classroom based practice.

Spencer et al. cite a more 'teacher-friendly' example of a school-based approach in the CCE literature review (2012b). Known as the *Creativity Wheel*[12] it was developed by a Creative Partnerships team in the Durham/Sunderland area and comprised 14 segments, each one representing an aspect of creative behaviour. Taking its cue from the definition of creativity promoted by the Qualifications and Curriculum Authority in England, creativity within the 'wheel' is understood as a combination of three facets: imagination with a purpose, value and originality.

Schools have also developed their own assessment tools to explore creative development, some of them from within the Creative Partnerships programme – one notable example being the trialled versions of an assessment tool used by Thomas Tallis School in London which, at the time of writing, are available on the school's website.[13] Craft et al.'s (2006) pilot study *Progression in Creative Learning*, also provides examples of school-based attempts at assessment through its exploration of ways of documenting and understanding progression from Foundation Stage through to Key Stage 4 in the subject areas English and Music.

The review by Spencer et al. does provide a more comprehensive survey of the range of assessment tools at the disposal of teachers and employers than is possible within the scope of this book, but suffice to say that when all the major approaches have been considered there is as yet no agreed upon framework, or standard tool for assessment of creativity for use in schools. While the Qualifications and Curriculum Authority's (QCA) (2004) *Creativity: Find it, promote it* document, offers some suggestions for noticing creativity, the list of observable behaviours is not amplified in QCA's subsequent chapter, 'How can you promote creativity?'. Instead, QCA focuses on informal assessment through pupil feedback and gathering evidence through video, audio, observation etc., as a means to further developing their creativity. This has the effect of offering teachers a way of noticing a set of attributes associated with creativity but no way of understanding how each might look as it develops, running the risk of engendering repeated 'entry level' activities.

Developing a new assessment tool

Having surveyed the literature the next step is to show some of the more teacher-friendly approaches to assessment and how a new assessment model was developed where a classroom-based observer was given an opportunity to use this information as a way of forward planning for individual learner's needs. The remainder of this chapter will describe this process, and share this new model, which at the time of writing is still in development.

Following on from the literature review, Spencer, Lucas and Claxton began the task of narrowing focus in order to develop an assessment tool that can be trialled. Five dimensions formed the basis of the model and were selected, as Spencer et al. (2012b) point out, for 'pragmatic reasons' (p. 38). These five dimensions provide a manageable number for teachers to focus on but still allows for some depth and precision conceptually. The dimensions selected are all drawn from aspects of creative behaviour that figure prominently in the literature review, two of which – 'Disciplined' and 'Collaborative' – have often been underrepresented in schools' approaches to creative learning. 'Discipline' draws on a literature around the development of expertise and the craft and skill elements of creativity. 'Collaborative' draws on literatures of communities of practice, communities of learning and social intelligence. The work of Lave and Wenger (1991) on communities of practice is a key reference point here.

As well as defining the conceptual heart of the assessment tool – the core elements of creativity which we will come on to shortly – Spencer et al.'s literature review also pointed us towards a tool that could assess a range of creative dispositions in the individual. This helpfully ruled out a number of other possibilities – the assessment of 'originality', present in the *Creativity Wheel*, for example. As Spencer et al. suggest:

> the notion of 'originality', while given importance by the NACCCE report (and others), was not focused upon further because of its relationship with the product, (which we were not assessing) rather than the person.
>
> (p. 42)

A number of other criteria for the tool became clear as direct result of the literature review and were set out by Spencer, et al. (2012) as follows:

- It was essential that an assessment framework should be useful to teachers. While it might involve peers, it would almost certainly involve the individual concerned in order to stimulate formative learning conversations.
- Relating to this first point, the framework should not attempt to be an exhaustive or definitive framework for describing the creative individual. Although making use of psychological constructs, the study should not involve statistical factor analysis or similar methods intended to attain a psychologically 'valid' profile. The study is concerned ultimately with utility.
- The tool must be useful to teachers who are interested in the 'learnability' of creative mindedness. This means it has to be at the right 'grain' of analysis;

not so abstract that teachers cannot easily see how they might address the learnability of each habit of mind; but not so fine-grained that the framework becomes unwieldy or unworkable.

- The terminology has to be clear, accessible, unambiguous, and have face validity with the target audience. With this in mind, we decided that 'habits' (creative dispositions) might best be described as adjectives, and sub-habits as 'gerunds' (verbal nouns, or action phrases). Abstract nominalisations might best be avoided.
- Consistent with teachers' expressed preferences, the tool must be applicable to a broad range of real-world types of creativity, including scientific and intellectual, visual and performing arts, and professions, including crafts and design.
- The framework should be as comprehensive as possible, covering all the most important creative qualities of mind. The elements of the framework should be as distinct as possible, having evidently different foci, and also being internally coherent, with the sub-habits showing a clearly understandable 'family relationship' to one other. The multiple realities and perspectives that users of a creativity framework will experience mean that a sense of total objectivity about terms cannot be claimed. Instead, the framework should hold to qualitative principles of trustworthiness, quality and rigour. Its terms should hold truth value; remaining intuitively distinct from one another and possessing confirmability as they are shown to be useful descriptors to both teachers and pupils. For teachers, face validity, demonstrated through the tools' usefulness in stimulating recognition and perception of creativity development in individuals, was of more significance.
- The framework should be consistent with previous policy and published research on creative traits.

(p. 36)

At the heart of this approach were five distinct, (and as the researchers hypothesised) learnable creative dispositions demonstrated by creative individuals and rooted in literatures describing their practice. The hypothesis was simple: recognition and development of these dispositions would allow individuals to become more creative within a particular context – in our case teachers and pupils within schools.

The Centre for Real-world Learning's background in learning science enabled the research team to draw on Costa and Kallick's work in the US (2000) which describes learning as a 'habit of effective thinking', rather than being about particular behaviours. The term 'habits of mind', first coined by Costa, has come to represent the sets of tendencies employed by learners at the right time to solve a problem. Claxton's own work (2002) in the UK has also identified a similar set of habits and Spencer et al. propose that this sort of approach can be used to develop creativity.

Five creative 'habits' of the creative mind

There are a range of potential habits that might be included within a broad definition of creativity and these are touched on in the literature review in greater detail. It was important that we isolated the key habits that would have greatest utility at the school level while being fundamental to the notion of creativity itself. After much discussion, Spencer et al. created a first model that comprised the following five core habits of the creative mind with a range of sub-habits delineated to provide the depth and richness required.

1 **Inquisitive.** Based on the premise that creative individuals are good at uncovering and pursing interesting and worthwhile questions in their creative domain.
   - Wondering and questioning
   - Exploring and investigating
   - Challenging assumptions

2 **Persistent.** Acknowledging the important role determination plays in creativity. The well-known 1 % inspiration, 99 % perspiration aphorism has been repeatedly emphasised in debates around creativity.
   - Sticking with difficulty
   - Daring to be different
   - Tolerating uncertainty

3 **Imaginative.** At the heart of a wide range of analyses of the creative personality is the ability to come up with imaginative solutions and possibilities
   - Playing with possibilities
   - Making connections
   - Using intuition

4 **Collaborative.** Many approaches to creativity place an emphasis on the social and collaborative nature of the process.
   - Sharing the product
   - Giving and receiving feedback
   - Cooperating appropriately

5 **Disciplined.** As a counterbalance to the 'blue sky thinking', imaginative side of creativity, many authors also note a requirement for knowledge and craft in shaping the creative product.
   - Developing techniques
   - Reflecting critically
   - Crafting and improving

The model tested at the initial stages of the research project is set out below. Detailed instructions were also made available to teachers as a way of aiding mediation of the model. These are reproduced in Appendix 6. The tool was designed in such a way that each of the 15 sub-habits could be assessed in relation to three dimensions:

- **strength:** the level of independence demonstrated by pupils in terms of their need for teacher prompts or scaffolding, or congenial conditions;
- **breadth:** the tendency of pupils to exercise creative dispositions in new contexts, or in a new domain;
- **depth**: the level of sophistication of disposition application and the extent to which application of dispositions was appropriate to the occasion.

The model was tested with the co-operation of a number of schools and through a combination of field notes and interviews we learned the following:

- We found that the particular multifaceted conception of creativity behind the tool, shown in its five 'habits' was seen as sufficiently inclusive by teachers.
- The division of each of the five 'habits' into three 'sub-habits' led to an assessment task that proved too onerous for teachers.
- As a proof of concept, Field Trail 1 showed us that the five 'habits' were sufficiently comprehensive, and that teachers were able to situate individual pupils on a tool that gauged the extent to which pupils had developed each habit.
- The tool's approach to progression as three dimensions 'strength', 'breadth', and

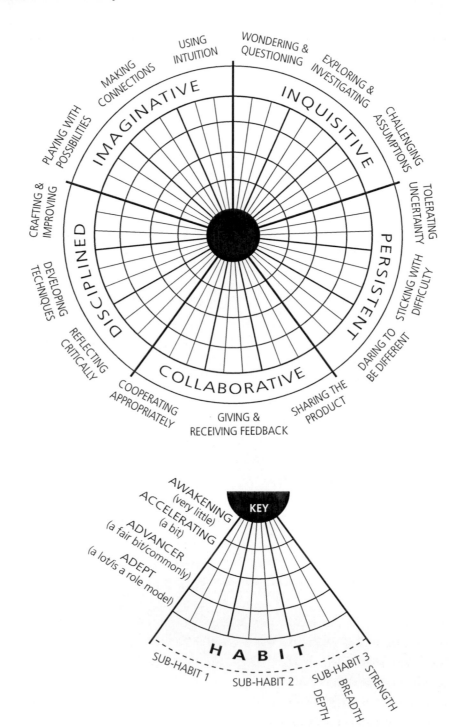

Figure 8.1 Progression in Creativity Tool, Version 1

'depth' was found to be an interesting one. In practice, however, the assessment task it generated was too burdensome and complex.

- Teachers adapted the circle and the grid, with varying degrees of success. Both were adapted to create more space for annotation, for example, but important aspects of the tool (strength, breadth, and depth) were omitted in one school.
- Various sources were used. As a 'snapshot' trial, teachers made use of existing knowledge of pupils in many cases.
- We found that some of the tool's language needs to be made more user-friendly.
- The model needed to take a lower grain of detail. As it stood it was too unwieldy for teachers to carry out assessment.
- We found the model needed its vocabulary to be more immediately self-explanatory.
- The model was clear in its use of adjectives for broad 'traits', and verbal nouns for its sub-habits.
- The model was applicable to a broad range of real-world types of creativity (it was trialled by teachers from a range of subject areas).
- We found that the model was comprehensive (no missing habits or sub-habits were identified).
- The model was internally coherent, with distinct elements (no overlap was identified).

Using the new model in your school or learning site

Adjusting the model and hearing back from teachers throughout a second phase of field trials left us with a clear sense of what might need to be developed further with this tool, and these points should certainly be kept in mind by any school or other learning site keen to try out this mode of assessment:

- The balance of simplicity and rigour is important. This project has attempted to span the gap between theory and practice, and has found that teachers will make best use of a tool that maintains this balance.
- The use of five habits is sufficiently detailed without being too unwieldy. The five habits we trialled were validated by practitioners and pupils and we think provide a useful means of staking out a territory or focus of inquiry.

The other clear finding was that the purpose of such an assessment tool, while needing to demonstrate its validity and rigour through a manageable number of constituent dispositions, also needed to avoid, at least at this early stage of development, any notion of grading or labelling pupils regarding their creativity. In keeping with this observation we found teachers reported a range of benefits of using the assessment tool. These related to:

- the potentially powerful use of feedback material for formative use by pupils;
- the additional focus and precision which our research-informed synthesis of five dispositions afforded teachers in their classroom activities;
- the influence of the tool on teachers, and its help in refining their practice, helping them to think specifically how they could cultivate the full range of creative dispositions;
- the boost to the status of creativity afforded by our clarification and refining of a practical, useful definition of creativity for those trying to argue its case. A more precise, research-led definition could be helpful in countering potentially negative impacts of a narrower curriculum upon creativity.

This leaves us at a stage in this project where further developments are required and we will continue to look at ways of making these happen. Any schools, educators, artists or others working in this field who may be interested in contributing to this development would be welcome to make use of this assessment tool, and to share any subsequent observations. The CCE and the Centre for Real World Learning plan to develop the assessment tool with the following priorities in mind:

- Maintaining the emphasis upon the *learnability* of creativity.
- Incorporating the tool into the school's data collection, reporting, and reward systems.
- Developing training materials and resources for teachers to demonstrate best practice, making the assessment process more tangible for teachers. Materials might relate to:
  - communicating the purpose;
  - linking evidence to the exemplar statement;
  - demonstrating the level of detail required;
  - preparing very young pupils.
- Developing layout to separate back out the three sub-habits of each creativity habit.
- Use of a clear design; easily decipherable by the youngest pupils.

- Scrutinising language to ensure it is sufficiently clear, particularly for younger children and those with special needs, but also those less familiar with creativity or learning vocabulary. This may mean creating different versions of the tool for different age groups.
- Developing best practice relating to how teachers might choose to focus on a small aspect of the tool at a time.
- Developing a more formative tool that prompts pupils and teachers to consider how they could improve, rather than just logging past behaviour. From a practical point of view, at present, the tool does not allow room for capturing progression adequately due to lack of space. Some pupils did date their notes, which showed progression to a small degree. Separation of the sub-habits would allow more focused notes on progression.
- Capturing 'breadth' more systematically in the tool, by establishing how it could be used in multiple contexts, and whether there would be any issues of ultimate ownership. This may involve exploring how schools best deal with the issue of co-ordination to ensure that assessments are undertaken systematically and collated in a useful format for both learners and teachers to use formatively. For example, schools may need to create and assign a co-ordinator role to ensure that assessments are undertaken. This role may fall naturally to the 'assessment co-ordinator' at primary level.
- Developing a more systematic evidence collection process. Developing materials to tackle teachers' thinking about the opportunities they provide in the curriculum.
- Developing the tool for the virtual environment.
- Trialling the tool with a broader range of schools and teachers, not only those who have previously expressed some commitment to the creativity agenda. In light of the fact that participating schools were a self-selecting group of 'keen' practitioners, the tool is yet to be exposed to the 'unconverted'. Its introduction to a group of schools unfamiliar with assessment of creativity would further test its practicality and utility.

This chapter has set out the early stages of development of a new model of assessment. The model is set out diagrammatically in Figure 8.1 and you can read about this model in more detail in the full research report by Spencer et al.[14]. Also available are notes and guidance materials which were were used during the field testing for this progression model. They may be useful to refer to when using this in classrooms and can be found in Appendix 6. These give an indication as to how this model was used in the research and how teachers might use it in future. However, it would be best to refer to the full report, where a more detailed account is given, if you intend to try to use the tool in your own teaching context.

Notes

1 This further amplified in Chapter 8 where the specific assessment of creative dispositions within individual learners is detailed.
2 For example, see 'The Aeroplane that became a Classroom' [at Kingsland Primary school in 2009]: http://www.guardian.co.uk/education/gallery/2009/mar/24/plane-classroom-school and 'Fasten your seatbelts children, your new geography classroom has landed in the playground': http://www.dailymail.co.uk/news/article–1165888/Fasten-seat-belts-children-new-geography-classroom-landed-playground.html>.
3 Reproduced with permission of CCE.
4 NOR: Number on roll
5 This is a tale of a food lover whose taste for extreme and revolting included large meals is depicted in lurid detail. Rufus' search for the ultimate in gruesome meals reaches a zenith in his attempt to make his own cake, the ingredients of which turn out to be so revoltingly powerful that the baked treat turns on its maker and tries to eat Rufus. He learns his lesson and becomes a very refined chef, eating delicately and healthily.
6 www.cceengland.org
7 www.artscouncil.org.uk
8 http://www.artscouncil.org.uk/what-we-do/our-priorities–2011–15/children-and-young-people/bridge-organisations/
9 http://www.queendom.com/queendom_tests/transfer
10 http://stupidstuff.org/main/creative01.htm
11 http://www.wherecreativitygoestoschool.com/Vancouver/left_right/rb_test.htm
12 http://www.creativejunction.org.uk/wp-content/uploads/creativity-wheel–127.pdf
13 http://creativetallis.blogspot.co.uk/2012/11/assessing-creativity.html
14 http://www.creativitycultureeducation.org/wp-content/uploads/Progression-in-Creativity-Final-Report-April–2012.pdf

Afterword: Creative Partnerships – The Future

The Creative Partnerships programme is no longer running in England but, at the time of writing, is beginning to be developed in other parts of the world. In this brief coda to the book we look forward to how schools and teachers in this country are keeping up the momentum for change and creativity in education, and how variants of the Creative Partnerships programme can emerge in other countries, being flexible to different contexts while remaining sharply defined in terms of its purpose and ambitions.

The previous chapter looked at the question of the assessment of creativity, particularly the challenge of 'progression'. Since progression will always involve a set of questions and speculations as to 'where next' for learners, it is also a useful concept when considering how the whole creativity agenda may develop. Where is creativity and creative learning headed in terms of policy and practice in education? Is it likely to be re-prioritised or given a new conceptual inflection of some sort, or both? And where might the appetite be within education for continued support for this way of working with young people?

Of course, it is impossible to be certain about the future shape of education policy and in some senses it is futile to speculate. However, there is increasing clarity on recent changes in the UK following the change of government in 2010.[1] Furthermore, if we are convinced that Creative Partnerships is a programme that led to a number of positive outcomes and that there is strong evidence, both empirical and anecdotal to support this, then we can strengthen the legacy that flows from that impact. We also have national studies using rigorous research methodologies to help to build our understanding of potential causal effects, as well as rich and descriptive accounts from individual projects. These combine to build a full account of the benefits of creative approaches to teaching and learning.

Creative Partnerships certainly achieved a great deal, and through research and practice has helped finesse an already long history of arts interventions and educational research, but there is still much to learn. If Creative Partnerships makes a contribution to our understanding of creative education it is in ways that both contest and confirm what we knew before.

The process of administering this large-scale programme led to an examination of assumptions about the nature and effect of creative practice; we were taken to places where practice and rhetoric sometimes strained to breaking point, and to others where they married up neatly and productively. It was noteworthy that many of the key moments boiled down to questions of language, or the lack of it, to describe in close detail the rich practices teachers and artists might continue to use in their daily work. The concern here is that in the education sector, an already densely populated rhetorical space, if you have no way of talking critically and reflectively about what you do and how it works, its practices and associated legacy can quickly fade away when national funding ends. Much of the work CCE continues to do is about responding to this challenge of developing a discourse that helps make the elements of creativity explicit and useable in professional development scenarios.

What needs to happen next? Creative Partnerships has shown that creative learning programmes can be managed and run in ways that imply an internal coherence and stability. But it would be dishonest not to acknowledge that there are still instances – some within Creative Partnerships, and others across the arts and cultural sector – where practice demonstrably does not directly address the learning potential of young people, and might be said to develop along other lines entirely, for example, audience development, therapeutic education or as a bolt-on counterbalance to a 'standards' dominated mode of teaching. The ways in which creative and arts activities are mediated is, therefore, key. Arguably, recent shifts in policy, both culturally and educationally in England, take us backwards rather than develop what Creative Partnerships started to exemplify. At the time of writing we are confronted, once again, by a model of education defined by a government that might broadly be described as traditionalist and 'back to basics' in approach. In terms of cultural policy for young people, and perhaps keeping in step with the preferred educational mode, there appears to be a return to the notion of a cultural canon, and a desirable or even optimal amount of exposure to pre-defined forms of art and expression that are linked to what we might term 'traditional' art forms or 'high culture'.

These factors notwithstanding there are encouraging signs that the momentum is building positively in at least three ways.

First, some countries and regions are beginning to acknowledge the need for reform, rather than simply improve the system we already have. Many have identified creativity as a key component of that process. Perhaps the best example of this is the European Union's Growth Strategy 'Europe 2020'.[2] On one hand there is an educational ambition across the EU that equates strongly with evidence of impact from the Creative Partnerships programme, for example, the aim for better educational attainment – in particular, the call to reduce school drop-out rates below 10 %. On the other hand there is, in concert with the educational aims of the EU, a heavy emphasis on innovation and the need for the next generation to be able to turn ideas into jobs. There is undoubtedly more work to be done within the EU and greater visibility needs to be given to creative education across the commission if such work is to be properly supported, but the rhetorical shifts seem to be taking place and conditions for creativity in education are becoming more favourable as a result.

A good example of this would be the recently established Lithuanian version of Creative Partnerships. 'Kūrybinės partnerystės' is a three-year programme in Lithuania and it is anticipated that a total of 100 schools will take part, engaging more than 4,000 pupils in creative learning projects. The programme is operated by the Education Development Centre in Lithuania and it builds directly on the foundations of Creative Partnerships in England, using a similar model of creative agents and artists to help build and carry forward a momentum for change in schools.

Second, many teachers appear to be resisting pressure to drop the creative approaches they have recently adopted in favour of a 'back to basics' or 'one-size-fits-all' system. Instead, they are beginning to argue for creativity to be added to the notion of what a basic educational entitlement should comprise. A recent example in England is the low take up of additional resources around the synthetic phonics approach to the teaching of reading. Currently, it is the case that any state-funded school with Key Stage 1 pupils have until March 2013 to claim up to £3,000 to purchase a range of teaching products and training from a catalogue of approved products and services to support the synthetic phonics approach. However, the Department for Education has noted the low level of take-up in some areas, including Central Bedfordshire, Bedford, Hull, Medway, Portsmouth, Luton and Sheffield. And in 20 Local Authorities, by February 2012, not a single school had booked training for their staff. Although there is no direct link between a resistance to synthetic phonics and a rise in creative approaches to teaching, it is indicative of a broader mood among teachers that might be characterised as one that reclaims professional autonomy in the face of pressure to teach in one way only. From within Creative Partnerships itself, many teachers indicated they felt they were in a position whereby it wasn't an option to 'turn back' to the ways their school had approached teaching and learning before. This came through particularly strongly in the research by McLellan et al. (2012). Galton, in particular, has a long track record of fieldwork in schools and was in a good position to 'take the temperature' in terms of the general mood of teachers. In an interim report for the well-being research project he reflected on differences he perceived:

> *Three of us were involved in a study of the lives of primary teachers which conducted surveys and follow-up case studies in 2002 and again in 2007. The results were reported in Galton and MacBeath (2008)[3]. ...[O]ver the period 2002–07 we found most teachers were compliant while unenthusiastic when delivering the National Curriculum. They complained about curriculum overload, the effects of having to teach to the test on pupils and the feeling that they were no longer trusted as professionals. One of those interviewed described the love of teaching as being, 'squashed' out of people (Galton & MacBeath, 2008:31). Furthermore, many teachers were resigned to things 'always being like this' (ibid, p. 42).*
>
> *Our first impression was that in all schools visited this pessimistic vocabulary of embattlement has changed to one where there is now frequent reference to spontaneity and creativity. Whether a CP activity or an initiative such as Forest Schools in a control has acted as the catalyst for this reversal, we found head teachers and their staff determined to exploit the newly gained freedoms in lesson planning even at the cost of defying the government should they seek to re-impose a subject based curriculum. This resilience has arisen in part from the changes in pupils when the curriculum is designed to promote active and meaningful learning. Many teachers spoke of having their expectations about the capabilities of pupils previously categorised as 'slow or difficult' being 'changed enormously.'*
>
> (McLellan and Galton, 2011, p. 7)

There was also a great deal of anecdotal evidence from teachers across Creative Partnerships captured in many of the school case studies set out earlier in this book, that they had, in effect, reached a point of no return. For them the prospect of going back to the way they had approached pedagogy before seemed unthinkable.

Third, and perhaps most importantly, many children are demanding an alternative approach. There is pressure building from young people, partly driven by the growing disconnection for many between their school lives and their social lives – experienced as growing 'gaps' of one sort or another. These include the uses and applications of technology, the kinds of discourses and approaches that define what 'learning' might be, rules that determine appropriate social interaction, the degree of agency and engagement elicited from tasks, set of values and overall ethos, indeed many of the aspects touched on directly or indirectly within the preceding chapters. All these seem to function one way outside of school for young people, and another way within it. Children notice this and respond accordingly (McLellan et al., 2012, provided compelling evidence of this), either inferring the unwritten rules and adopting them, becoming apathetic towards school and switching off, or, as we increasingly found within schools participating in Creative Partnerships, bouncing back the contradictions to the school and expecting a better solution. There is also a growing realisation amongst those young people who have been participants within programmes such as Creative Partnerships, that there are viable alternatives that they can help design and deliver themselves, thereby fulfilling their needs to be agents in the process, determining for themselves how they can improve and develop. We saw this reflected in the school case studies earlier, and in the research by Galton (2008) and McLellan et al. (2012) in particular.

Throughout the preceding chapters we have seen compelling evidence to suggest a programme of creative education, driven by a pedagogy underpinned by attributes of creative people, can fulfil the needs of the education system as it is currently configured. But more than this, it can prepare young people in ways that best anticipate the likely needs of the future. It does this by developing the kinds of skills broadly agreed to be relevant and appropriate for the twenty-first century. A good example of this is a set of principles formulated by the UNESCO Task Force on Education for the Twenty-first Century. These principles are expressed as four essential pillars: learning to know, learning to do, learning to live together and learning to be.[4] Creative Partnerships always recognised that learning to know (the acquisition of knowledge) and learning to do (the development of technical skills) are central to education and they were often at the heart of a school's application to join the programme. However, to require formal education to limit itself to just these two areas is becoming ever more damaging to young people. This is because the essential skills necessary for future success are predicated as much on the development of social and creative abilities as the acquisition of facts and technical skills. And since there is no conflict between them, something we have demonstrated throughout this book, it is for many young people the equivalent of significant lost opportunity that schools are required to offer an education based on only half the principles set out by UNESCO.

For this reason, Creative Partnerships, and the kinds of legacies it leaves need to be championed and nurtured. This will include new versions of the programme in other countries, the research and academic papers it provokes, through to the less formal store of experiences and expertise developed amongst the teachers, young people and creative professionals who were part of the programme. This book is a contribution to that process. It is a reminder that creative learning continues to develop and grow and is a way of working that can be embedded in any school.

Notes

1 Generally, we are seeing changes to policy that place creativity and the arts under threat. The ongoing development of the English Baccalaureate, a proposed measure that recognises where pupils have secured a C grade or better across a core of academic subjects – English, mathematics, history or geography, the sciences and a language – implicitly places arts subjects in a lower tier. It perpetuates old dichotomies which prevailed over 40 years ago, before the Plowden report (1967), the idea that the arts are not about learning directly, and much more about pleasure, thereby potentially distracting from the central business of schooling.

2 http://ec.europa.eu/europe2020/index_en.htm

3 Galton, M. and MacBeath, J. (2008) *Teachers Under Pressure,* London: Sage Publications.

4 http://www.unesco.org/delors/fourpil.htm

References

Amabile, T., Conti, R., Coon, H., Lazenby, J. and Herron, M. (1996), 'Assessing the Work Environment for Creativity', *Academy of Management Journal,* 39(5): 1154-1184.

Banaji, S., Burn, A. and Buckingham, D. (2010), 'The Rhetorics of Creativity: A Literature Review' (2nd edition). Newcastle: Creativity, Culture and Education (CCE). Available at: http://www.creativitycultureeducation.org/the-rhetorics-of-creativity-a-literature-review

Bentley, T. and Seltzer, K. (1999), *The Creative Age*. DEMOS: London.

BOP Consulting. (2012), 'School Case Studies', in *Changing Young Lives*. Newcastle: CCE.

Blunt, C. (2004), *Agents in Change*. London: Creative Partnerships, Arts Council England.

Bragg, S. and Manchester, H. (2011), 'Creativity, School Ethos and the Creative Partnerships programme'. CCE: Newcastle.

Brice Heath, S. and Wolf, S. (2004), *Visual Learning in the Community School*. Kent: Creative Partnerships, Arts Council England. Available at: http://www.creativitycultureeducation.org/visual-learning-in-the-community-school

Brice Heath, S. and Wolf, S. (2005), *Visual Learning in the Community School*. London: Creative Partnerships.

Bruner, J. (1960), *The Process of Education*. Cambridge, MA: Harvard University Press.

Bruner, J. (1996), *The Culture of Education*. Cambridge, MA: Harvard University Press.

Central Advisory Council for Education. (1967), 'Children and their Primary Schools: The Plowden Report'. HMSO: London.

Creativity Culture Education (CCE). (2012), 'Changing Young Lives: Research Digest 2006 – 2012' in *Changing Young Lives*. Newcastle: CCE.

Claxton, G. (2002), *Building Learning Power*. Bristol: TLO Limited.

Cooper, L., Benton, T. and Sharp, C. (2011), 'The Impact of Creative Partnerships on Attainment and Attendance in 2008-9 and 2009-10'. Slough: NFER. https://www.creativitycultureeducation.org/the-impact-of-creative-partnerships-on-attainment-and-attendance-in-2008-9-and-2009-10

Cooperrider, D. and Whitney, D. (2005), *Appreciative Inquiry: A positive revolution in change*. San Fransisco, CA: Berrett-Koehler Publishers Inc.

Costa, A. and Kallick, B. (2000), *Habits of Mind: A developmental series*. Alexandria, VA: Association for Supervision and Curriculum Development.

Craft, A., Burnard, P., Grainger, T. and Chappell, K. (2006) *Progression in Creative Learning*. London: Arts Council England, Creative Partnerships. Available at: http://www.creativitycultureeducation.org/progression-in-creative-learning

Cropley, A. J. (2001), *Creativity in Education and Learning: A Guide for Teachers and Educators*. London: Routledge.

Csikszentmihalyi, M. (1991), *Flow: The psychology of optimal experience*. London: Harper.

Cutler, Anna (2010), 'What Is To Be Done, Sandra? Learning in Cultural Institutions of the

Twenty-First Century', *Tate Papers*, Spring. Available at: http://www.tate.org.uk/research/publications/tate-papers/what-be-done-sandra-learning-cultural-institutions-twenty-first

Desforges, C. and Abouchaar, A. (2003), 'The Impact of Parental Involvement, Parental Support and Family Education on Pupil Achievements and Adjustment: A Literature Review'. London: Department for Education and Skills.

Durbin, B., Rutt, S., Saltini, F., Sharp, C., Teeman, D. and White, K. (2010), 'The Impact of Creative Partnerships on School Attainment and Attendance: Final Report'. Newcastle: CCE. Available at: http://www.creativitycultureeducation.org/impact-of-creative-partnerships-on-young-peoples-behaviour-and-attainment-2010

Eames, A., Benton, T. Sharp, C and Kendall, L. (2006), 'The Longer Term Impact of Creative Partnerships on the Attainment of Young People: Final Report'. London: Arts Council England, Creative Partnerships. Available at: http://www.creativitycultureeducation.org/the-longer-term-impact-of-creative-partnerships-on-the-attainment-of-young-people

Ellis, S. and Safford, K. (2005), *Animating Literacy; inspiring children's learning through teacher and artist partnerships*. London: CLPE and Creative Partnerships, Arts Council England.

Fillis, I. and McAuley, A. (2000), 'Modeling and Measuring Creativity at the Interface', *Journal of Marketing Theory and Practice*, 8:2 (8-17).

Fleming, M. (2010), 'Arts in Education and Creativity: A Literature Review'. (2nd edition). Newcastle: CCE. Available at: http://www.creativitycultureeducation.org/arts-in-education-and-creativity-a-literature-review

Galton, M. (2006), 'The Pedagogy of Creative Practitioners in School: Final Report'. London: Arts Council England, Creative Partnerships. Available at: http://www.creativitycultureeducation.org/the-pedagogy-of-creative-practitioners-in-schools

Harland, J., Lord, P., Stott, A., Kinder, K., Lamont, E. and Ashowrth, M. (2005), 'The Arts Education Interface: A Mutual Learning Triangle?' .Slough: NFER.

Jones, K. (2009), 'Culture and Creative Learning: a literature review'. Newcastle: CCE. Available at: http://www.creativitycultureeducation.org/culture-and-creative-learning-a-literature-review

Kendall, L., Morrison, J., Sharp, C. and Yeshanew, T. (2008a), 'The Impact of Creative Partnerships on Pupil Behaviour: Final Report'. Slough: NFER. Available: http://www.nfer.ac.uk/nfer/publications/CPW01/CPW01.pdf

Kendall, L.; Morrison, J., Yeshanew, T. and Sharp, C. (2008b), 'The Longer-term Impact of Creative Partnerships on the Attainment of Young People: Results from 2005 and 2006. Final Report'. Slough: NFER. Available: http://www.nfer.ac.uk/nfer/publications/CPY01/CPY01.pdf

Lamont, E., Jeffes, J. and Lord, P. (2010), 'Evaluation of the nature and impact of the Creative Partnerships Programme on the teaching workforce'. Slough: NFER.

Lave, J. and Wenger, E. (1991). *Situated Learning: Legitimate peripheral participation*. Cambridge: Cambridge University Press.

McLellan, R. and Galton, M. (2011), The Impact of Creative Partnerships on Student Well-being: Interim Report, February 2011. Unpublished, Creativity, Culture and Education.

McLellan, R., Galton, M., Steward, S., and Page, C. (2012), 'The impact of Creative Partnerships on the well-being of children and young people'. Newcastle: Creativity, Culture and Education.

NACCCE (National Advisory Committee on Creative and Cultural Education), (1999), *All Our Futures: Creativity Culture and Education*. London: DfEE and DCMS

Ofsted, (2001). Education Action Zones: Commentary on the First Six Inspections, Ofsted, London.

Parker, D. and Ruthra-Rajan, N. (2011), 'The Challenges of Developing System-Wide indicators of Creativity Reform: The Case of Creative Partnerships, UK' in J, Sefton-Green, P. Thomson, K. Jones and L. Bresler (eds), *The Routledge International Handbook of Creative Learning*. London: Routledge, pp. 448-458.

Plucker, J. and Makel, M. (2010) 'Assessment of Creativity' in J. Kaufman and R. Sternberg (eds.) *The Cambridge Handbook of Creativity*. Cambridge: Cambridge University Press, pp. 48 – 73.

Qualifications and Curriculum Authority (2004), *Creativity: Find it, promote it*. London: Qualifications and Curriculum Authority.

Robinson, K. (1982), *The Arts in Schools: Principles, practice and provision*. First edition. Calouste Gulbenkian Foundation: London.

Robinson, K. (2001), *Out of Our Minds: Learning To Be Creative*. Oxford: Capstone Publishing.

Safford, K. and Barrs, M. (2005), *Creativity and Literacy: Many Routes to Meaning: children's language and literacy learning in creative arts work*. London: CLPE. Available at: http://www.clpe.co.uk/research/creativity-projects

Safford, K. and O'Sullivan, O. (2007), '"Their learning becomes your journey": Parents respond to children's work with Creative Partnerships'. London: Arts Council England, Creative Partnerships. Available at: http://www.creativitycultureeducation.org/their-learning-becomes-your-journey-parents-respond-to-childrens-work-in-creative-partnerships

Seltzer, K and Bentley, T. (1999), 'The Creative Age: Knowledge and Skills for the New Economy'. London: DEMOS. Available at: http://www.demos.co.uk/publications/creativeage

Sefton-Green, J. (2008), 'Creative Learning', Arts Council, London

Spencer, E., Lucas, B. and Claxton, G. (2012a), 'Progression in Creativity: Developing New Forms of Assessment'. Newcastle: CCE. Available at: http://www.creativitycultureeducation.org/progression-in-creativity-developing-new-forms-of-assessment

Spencer, E., Lucas, B. and Claxton, G. (2012b), 'Progression in Creativity: A Literature Review'. Newcastle: CCE. Available at: http://www.creativitycultureeducation.org/progression-in-creativity-a-literature-review

Thomson, P. Hall, C., Jones, K. and Sefton-Green, J. (2012), 'The Signature Pedagogies Project: Final Report'. Newcastle: CCE. Available at: http://www.creativitycultureeducation.org/the-signature-pedagogies-project

Thomson, P., Jones, K. and Hall, C. (2009), 'Creative School Change'. Newcastle: CCE. Available at: http://www.creativitycultureeducation.org/creative-school-change

Trilling, B. and Fadel, C. (2009), *21st century skills: learning for life in our times*. San Francisco, CA: Jossey-Bass.

Appendix 1
Creative Partnerships 2002 – 2011: Key Facts and Figures

Funding

Total Funding – approximately £318m between 2001/2002 – 2011/2012. This was largely from Department for Culture, Media and Sport but included £2.5m from the Department for Education each year.

Dates of activity in schools

May 2002 – August 2011

Numbers – national figures[1]

Total number of schools taking part in Creative Partnerships between 2002 – 2011: 5,324
Percentage of schools in England that took part in Creative Partnerships: 21.72%[2]
Total number of young people taking part 2002 – 2008: 940,479
Total number of young people taking part 2008 – 2011: 790,350
Total number of teachers taking part 2002 – 2008: 90,536
Total number of teachers taking part 2008 – 2011: 61,009

Appendix 2
Discussing the Rhetorics of Creativity – Prompt Questions from Banaji et al. (2010)

Reproduced from Banaji et al. (2010, pp. 73–74) with permission from CCE.

These questions are presented by Banaji et al. (2010) to aid discussions by school staff and stakeholders about the different uses of the word 'creativity' and the implications of those different uses for school policies, curriculum and activities.

1. Is creativity an internal cognitive function, or is it an external social and cultural phenomenon?

- Does creativity come from nowhere, a lateral or spontaneous insight, or is it dependent on incremental transformations of familiar genres and templates? Is 'imagination' the lone endeavour of inspired individuals, or a social, collaborative design process?
- What is the relationship between cultural learning and creative learning? While some of the rhetorics conceive of creativity without reference to culture, others conceive of all creativity as irreducibly cultural; and, furthermore, that the arts naturalise the cultural values of dominant social groups. How can creative learning projects take this kind of cultural politics into account?
- How can cultural consumption be connected to 'creative' production?
- How does creative production draw on people's cultural experiences as audiences, readers, spectators, players?
- How can creative learning programmes connect children's experience of the arts, both within and beyond school, with the opportunity for them to become creative producers?

2. Is creativity a pervasive, ubiquitous feature of human activity, or a special faculty, either reserved for particular groups, individuals, or particular domains of activity, in particular artistic activity?

- How might democratic accounts of creativity, which avoid the problem of elitism, nevertheless accommodate notions of exceptional talent?
- To what extent does creativity mean the same thing in arts and non-arts contexts and how is this term helpful in these different settings? On the one hand, many educators want to argue the case for an everyday creativity, implicit in every child's every act and utterance, and for creativity in all curriculum areas. On the other hand, while no-one could reasonably deny that science and maths have their own forms of creative thinking, is there something specific about work that self-consciously constitutes itself as 'art', which requires a more specific definition, related to forms of aesthetic effect and judgment?

3. Is creativity an inevitable social good, invariably progressive, harmonious and collaborative; or is it capable of disruption, political critique and dissent, and even anti-social outcomes?

- Arts curricula and arts education projects emphasise positive social benefits and a collaborative ideal. But what of expressions of creativity that do not fit in with current social definitions of acceptable collective social endeavour; that are, perhaps, individualist, anti-social, troubling and even dangerous? Such expressions recall popular notions of the artist as tormented individual, or the artist as political critic.
- Is creativity political, and if so, how? The creative work of young people can clearly have explicitly political purposes, or can represent implicitly political impulses. How can these potentials be recognised, developed, encouraged? What happens when they collide with institutional values or protocols?

4. What does the notion of creative teaching and learning imply?

- What is the difference between 'good' pedagogy and 'creative' pedagogy? How is creative teaching and learning different from 'good' or 'effective' teaching and 'engaged' or 'enthusiastic' learning? What is the added value of using the term 'creativity' in this context?

- How is creative learning related to play? Notions of creativity as hard work, skills-based, and ultimately a preparation for the adult workplace, can be opposed to notions of 'game-based learning' which propose a wholesale critique of learning as joyless, mechanistic work, and contrasting it with dynamic forms of learning seen to reside in play. In addition, different theories can represent children's play as, on the one hand, progressive, rule-governed and socially beneficial, and on the other hand as chaotic and risky, echoing similar contradictions within theories of creativity.

Appendix 3
Creative Learning – Big Paper Training Exercise and Examples of Outcomes

The following is based on a simple exercise devised by Anna Cutler (former Director of Creative Partnerships) to kick off training sessions about the creative learning evaluation model being piloted in 2005–06 and which is set out in Chapter 2. It was designed to allow delegates to break down the concept of creativity in a way that was of practical use when planning and reflecting on classroom activities.

This exercise is good for engaging a large amount of people in the same thinking. We have used it to explore and come to an agreement on people's understandings of the terms referred to in 'DOING' and 'SHOWING' of the Creative Learning Model.

What to do

1 You will need 14 pieces of flipchart paper and as many fat big felt pens as there are people joining in.
2 Write down the seven different aspects of DOING and SHOWING, one as a title on each piece of paper as follows:
   - DOING: Problem Identification
   - DOING: Divergent Thinking
   - DOING: Taking Risks
   - DOING: Balance of Skills and Challenges
   - DOING: Co-learning
   - DOING: Fascination
   - DOING: Refinement
   - SHOWING: Solving Problems
   - SHOWING: New Ideas
   - SHOWING: Confidence
   - SHOWING: New Skills

- SHOWING: Capacity to Learn
- SHOWING: Engagement
- SHOWING: Valued Outcome

3 Blue-tack these pages around the walls or lay them out on tables before your group arrives.

4 Ask all involved to write on each piece of paper what they understand the title to mean/be/look like in a classroom/educational setting. This can be one sentence or a few words. Copying is definitely allowed and spelling is unimportant – explain this.

5 This exercise usually takes 15 to 20 minutes and is usually completed in silence because people are thinking but it doesn't matter if they talk.

6 After everyone has finished (there is often a natural pause, but create one after 20 minutes if they are still writing) take one sheet and analyse what people have said, read it out and look at what key words and ideas appear on the page.

7 Ask them to come up with one sentence that they feel encapsulates the key ideas and words on the page.

8 Get them to repeat this in smaller groups if you have time, so that eventually you have 14 separate sentences that describe the '14 Creative Learning Features' – all done by the group. If you don't have time to do this, it doesn't matter as the key thinking will have been done and you can write up the ideas and send them back to everyone for reference.

Examples of delegates' responses

The following sentences are a record of delegates' responses to Anna Cutler's presentations on evaluation and creative learning in November 2005.

Problem Identification

- Discussion, working co-operatively
- Taking time to observe and think
- Not being content with how things are
- Finding the language to articulate thought
- Seeking problems – seeing them as fun!
- Using the words to describe the problem
- Not always a right or wrong way

- I can't do it! How do I do it?
- Analysing and questioning
- I am stuck! What now?
- Cognitive thinking
- Experience a challenge

Divergent Thinking

- Can I try it this way, Miss?
- Putting together the seemingly unconnected
- I think it'll work if I try it this way instead
- I thought it would be better this way
- Trying something new, or just different
- What if?...Being inquisitive
- Children knowing how they can learn best e.g. recording in different ways
- Twelve ways to use a chair without sitting on it
- Taking different approaches – not just following one line of thought because it is known to work
- Global awareness
- Doing something new
- Using a variety of knowledge from a variety of subject areas
- Originality – surprising thoughts, views and opinions

Taking Risks

- Being in a safe environment and feeling safe before taking any type of risk
- Great idea, now go for it
- Working easily with all peers – even the ones you thought you didn't like
- No pressure!
- Putting a hand up and asking questions
- Trying something new (or again/or old)
- Not worrying about failure
- Sometimes being prepared to destroy, in order to create
- Not being afraid
- Confidence
- Being first to go ahead
- Doing something never attempted before
- Being confident in failure

- If you think you can…
  - Positive attitude

Balance of Skills and Challenges

- Something for every child – full engagement
- Showing improvement
- I didn't think I was good enough to do that – but I did!
- Children willing to have a go
- Children challenging each other
- Equality of all abilities
- Asking how to get better
- Cross curriculum working
- Self challenge
- Small achievable steps
- Variety of tasks to give a broad range of skills and challenges
- Equality of all abilities
- Questioning
- Knowing and daring

Co-learning

- Students interrupting with ideas for tasks
- Exchanging thoughts and ideas together
- Students happy to show the teacher how to do it
- Helping each other
- Communicating
- Children asking other children for help
- Being 'wrong' together
- Asking how, what and why questions
- Practicing together
- Working with outside businesses, schools, adults and international links
- Delving into the unknown together
- Role reversal: students as teachers, teachers as students
- Teachers and pupils delighting in new thinking

Fascination

- Completely involved and absorbed in the activity
- Asking questions
- Lost in thought
- Can't wait to get to it/find out
- Excitement, enjoyment and pride
- Enthusiasm and excitement
- Completely immersed in the task
- Not hearing the instruction to stop
- Concentration
- A thirst to learn more
- Continuing at home/out of school and bringing in the result

Refinement

- Accepting it might not be right first time
- Attention to detail
- Satisfaction from skills gradually improving
- How do I make it better?
- Self evaluation and determination
- Why does this not work? How do I improve it?
- Practise
- Wanting to have another go
- Having the confidence to make improvements
- Not being afraid to amend or review – continual reflection
- Questioning
- Comparing with work from before
- Offering to do more

Solving Problems

- Asking questions and giving explanations
- Accepting mistakes
- Being self-critical
- Clear thinking about the necessary steps to take to reach a solution
- Working collaboratively – discussing and planning solutions to problems
- Finding the key words

- Seeing patterns to provide solutions
- Having a shared goal
- Demonstrating your (practical) achievement
- Employing strategies and skills for learning already previously identified
- Teamwork – sharing of ideas
- Open minded thinking
- Knowing how to think through an idea

New Ideas

- Using different media
- If I do it this way, will I get the same result?
- Being controversial with ideas
- Children having their own opinions, not just accepting those of parents, teachers and peers
- Not worrying about failure
- Excitement and confidence
- Now I want to know what happens when…Let's find out.
- Embracing new projects
- Asking questions and tangential thinking
- Investigating and exploring – I wonder why?

Confidence

- Asking questions, giving explanations
- Accepting mistakes
- Being self-critical
- Sharing willingly
- Helping other students
- Willing to take risks – to question the value of learning
- Volunteering
- Happy to go wrong in front of other students
- Being imaginative
- Happy
- Answering a question and not being afraid of giving the wrong answer
- Knowing yourself: high value on intra-personal talents
- Changes in body language and mannerisms
- Questioning themselves and others
- I know what you said, but I think it would be better if…. Is that ok?

New Skills

- Now I understand, I'm ready to move on…
- Involved in new activities, developing and learning completely new skills
- Applying skills to other areas – practising them
- Choosing a different way of doing something
- Transference of skills
- Achievement and success
- Pride
- I couldn't do that before, Miss
- Demonstrating to others
- Being able to transfer to peers, re-enforcing confidence and risk taking abilities
- Using skills in diverse ways
- Spinning gold from straw
- Having the tools to tackle a task in a variety of ways

Capacity to Learn

- Showing you can have a 'go' working independently
- Using past learning in new contexts
- Improvement as a result of feedback
- Adjusting own view after listening to the view of another
- Being open to new ideas
- Asking questions
- Comfortable with surroundings and the people involved
- Living/surviving
- Improved confidence and self-esteem
- Feeling safe
- Ability to help someone else
- Security in the environment and within themselves
- Developing strategies to embrace challenging tasks

Engagement

- Enthusiasm
- Focus
- All children and adults involved in the learning process
- Deep thought

- It can't be time to stop!
- Chatting about the task in hand
- Deep involvement – taking the idea further
- Whole school enthusiasm
- Wanting to repeat or continue the activity
- Absorption
- Happy to go to school
- Discussing school outside of school
- Interest and enjoyment
- Planning and setting out a 'vision'
- Eyes wide open

Valued Outcome

- Pride – wanting to share
- Exhibition
- Taking home to show and showing others
- Positive and proud
- Asking can we do it again?
- Achievement
- Repeatedly talking about their achievement
- Praise
- Performance
- Constructive criticism and positive feedback
- Pleased with the results
- Other children/adults responding to how well something went – picking out positive features
- Something to build on

Appendix 4
Evaluation – Creative Learning Forms

Four creative learning forms are provided in this section (see Chapter 2 for discussion of their use):

- Creative Learning Record Sheet
- Questionnaire – Cultural Practitioners
- Questionnaire – Teachers
- Questionnaire – Young People

Creative Learning Record Sheet

Please complete a new form for each individual interviewed

TEACHER TCH [   ]

CULTURAL PRACTITIONER CP [   ]

OTHER [   ]

Project title _____

School name _____

Interviewee NACME_____

Number of young people involved in project _____

Year group of young people involved in project _____

Any other information (i.e. context of school or particularity of project):

INPUT

KEY: 0 = no value 1 = some value   2 = good value   3 = significant value
TCH= Teacher   CP= Cultural Practitioner   YP=Young People

Fill in two boxes, one for the interviewee and one concerning the young people.

INPUT Before	TCH	YP	Priority	Record comments to 'why' here
Idea				
Language				
Environment				
Resources				
Qualities and Values				

INPUT After	TCH	YP	Priority	Record comments to 'why' here
Idea				
Language				
Environment				
Resources				
Qualities and Values				

DOING

In the Process of DOING the project have you observed any change in the following?

Please fill in two boxes, one for the interviewee and one concerning the young people.

KEY: 0 = no change 1 = small change 2 = clear change 3 = radical change

DOING	TCH	CP	YP	Comments and Quotes Please account for what changes and why
1. Identifying Problems				
2.Divergent Thinking				
3. Co-Learning				
4. Fascination				
5. Risk Taking				
6. Balance Skills vs Challenge				
7. Refinement				

SHOWING

As a result of doing the project have you observed any change in what can be shown?

Please fill in two boxes, one for the interviewee and one concerning the young people.

KEY: 0 = no change 1 = small change 2 = clear change 3 = radical change

SHOWING	TCH	CP	YP	Comments and Quotes Please account for what changes and why
1. Problem solving				
2. New Ideas				
3. Capacity to Learn				
4. Engagement				
5. Confidence				
6. New Skills				
7. Purposeful Outcomes				

REFLECTION

When reflecting on what you/the young people have both done and shown, what do you think were the key outcomes for:

You
The young people
The school community more broadly
What would you do differently next time?
Were there any surprising/unexpected outcomes?

Signed interviewer _____

Interviewee _____

Date _____

Questionnaire – Cultural Practitioners

Your name [   ]

Project name [   ]

DOING: During the process of the CP project this term:

On a sliding scale of 0 – 3 with 3 at the highest value and 0 the lowest have you…

1 …used this opportunity with CP to identify and address particular ideas/ issues/ challenges?

$$0-1-2-3$$

> *What are these? If not, what is the project seeking to do?*

2 …asked questions and challenged assumptions through the project?

$$0-1-2-3$$

> *If yes, please give examples*

3   ...learned alongside the young people and adults involved?

0 — 1 — 2 — 3

> *If yes, please give examples, if not, why do you think you didn't?*

4   ... been motivated through your own curiosity of the project subject matter?

0 — 1 — 2 — 3

> *Please indicate how or explain why this hasn't been the case*

5   ...taken any positive risks during the course of CP?

0 — 1 — 2 — 3

> *Please give examples or explain why this hasn't been the case*

6 ...gained any new skills?

$$0 - 1 - 2 - 3$$

> *Please give examples if any, or explain why this hasn't been the case*

6a ...had your artistic practice stretched within your work in the school?

$$0 - 1 - 2 - 3$$

> *If yes, please indicate how*

7 ...had the chance to refine your work?

$$0 - 1 - 2 - 3$$

> *If yes, please give examples*

As a result of doing the project what has been SHOWN:

On a sliding scale of 0 – 3 with 3 at the highest value and 0 the lowest have you...

1 ...sought new challenges and been engaged in problem solving through the project?

$$0 - 1 - 2 - 3$$

What did this look like in practice?

2 ...had any new ideas yourself emerging from this project?

$$0 - 1 - 2 - 3$$

If yes, how have you communicated these? If not, why do you think this is the case?

3 ...found yourself learning new things with young people and adults?

$$0 - 1 - 2 - 3$$

> *If yes, what did this look like – was it enjoyable and did it look different from when you work alone?*

4 ...found that your engagement with the CP Project has been more than in other projects?

$$0 - 1 - 2 - 3$$

> *If yes, please indicate how*

5   ...gained increased confidence through the CP project?

$$0 - 1 - 2 - 3$$

> *Was this about your own work or the work in schools or both/neither? If neither, please explain why not*

6   ...gained any new skills through the project?

$$0 - 1 - 2 - 3$$

> *If yes, what are these?*

7 ...produced any concrete work with those involved (performance/exhibition/made object) that you consider to be of high or low value?

$$0 - 1 - 2 - 3$$

What was it and why does it have good/some/no value? If not, what outcome did you wish to produce?

Were there any unexpected outcomes?

What using the information above, would you say is the distance travelled from the beginning of this project until now?

What would you do differently if you did this project again?

Questionnaire – Teachers

Your name

Project name

DOING : During the process of the CP project this term

On a sliding scale of 0 – 3 with 3 at the highest value and 0 the lowest have you...

1 ...used this opportunity with CP to identify and address particular ideas/ issues/ challenges through the project?

$$0 - 1 - 2 - 3$$

What are these? If not, please explain why you think not

2 ...been challenged to look at things differently and ask questions?

$$0 - 1 - 2 - 3$$

Please give examples if you have. If not, why do you think you haven't?

3   ...learned alongside the young people and adults involved?

$$0 - 1 - 2 - 3$$

Please give examples if you have, if not, please indicate why you think not

4   ...been positively motivated by the project. Has it been of high or low interest to you?

$$0 - 1 - 2 - 3$$

Please indicate how or why/not

5 ... taken any positive risks during the course of CP?

$$0 - 1 - 2 - 3$$

What were these? If not, please explain why you think not

6 ... gained new skills?

$$0 - 1 - 2 - 3$$

Please give examples. If not, please explain why you think you haven't

6b ...wanted to change the approach to some areas of teaching and learning during this project?

$$0 - 1 - 2 - 3$$

If yes, please indicate how

7 ...had the opportunity to refine your work beyond the life of the CP project?

$$0 - 1 - 2 - 3$$

If yes please give examples, if not, please give examples why not

As a result of doing the project what has been SHOWN:

On a sliding scale of 0 – 3 with 3 at the highest value and 0 the lowest have you…

1 …found any solutions to the challenges posed at the outset of this project?

0 — 1 — 2 — 3

Please indicate how/why not

2 …had any new ideas yourself emerging from this project?

0 — 1 — 2 — 3

If yes, please say how have you communicated these

3 ...found yourself learning new things with young people and Cultural Practitioners?

$$0 - 1 - 2 - 3$$

> *What did this look like? If not, why do you think you didn't*

4 ...gained increased confidence in terms of creative approaches in the classroom?

$$0 - 1 - 2 - 3$$

> *If yes, please indicate how*

5 ...had new ideas and been able to share them with the practitioner, colleagues and pupils?

$$0 - 1 - 2 - 3$$

How has this been demonstrated?

6 ...sought new challenges during this project?

$$0 - 1 - 2 - 3$$

Please give examples

7   How important is the final outcome of this project?

$$0 - 1 - 2 - 3$$

How has this affected your work? If not, why do you think it has been of low importance?

Were there any unexpected outcomes?

What, using the information above, would you say is the distance travelled from the beginning of this project until now?

What would you do differently if you did this project again?

Questionnaire – Young People

Your name

Project name

DOING: During the process of the CP project this term

On a sliding scale of 0 – 3 with 3 at the highest value and 0 the lowest have young people…

1   …used this opportunity with CP to identify and address particular ideas/ issues/ challenges?

0 — 1 — 2 — 3

What are these? If not, why do you think they didn't?

2   …been encouraged to look at things differently and ask questions?

0 — 1 — 2 — 3

Please give examples if yes, if not, why do you think they didn't?

3 ...learned alongside the cultural practitioners and teachers involved?

0 — 1 — 2 — 3

Please give examples if you have and explain what the result was, if not, please indicate why you think not

4 ...been positively motivated by this project?

0 — 1 — 2 — 3

Please indicate how, if not, why do you think this is the case?

5 …taken any positive risks during the course of CP? (i.e. speaking out, taking the lead)

$$0 - 1 - 2 - 3$$

If yes, please give examples, if not, why do you think this is the case?

6 …acquired new skills/new language from the CP practitioner?

$$0 - 1 - 2 - 3$$

Please indicate how, if yes, if not, why do you think this is the case?

6a ...been given new challenges by the CP practitioner?

$$0 - 1 - 2 - 3$$

If yes, please indicate how. If not, what did the project seek to achieve for the young people?

7 ...had the opportunity to refine their work on their own or with the CP practitioner and/or the teachers?

$$0 - 1 - 2 - 3$$

Please give examples if yes, if not, why has this been the case?

As a result of doing the project what has been SHOWN

On a sliding scale of 0 – 3 with 3 at the highest value and 0 the lowest have young people…

1 …been able to find solutions or realised an idea in response to the particular ideas/issues/ challenges offered in this project?

$$0 - 1 - 2 - 3$$

> *Please indicate how if yes, if not, why not?*

2 …had new ideas and been able to share them with their friends, teacher, practitioner?

$$0 - 1 - 2 - 3$$

> *If yes, how has this been demonstrated?*

3 ...appeared to have learned more quickly or enjoyed the learning process more than you would usually expect?

$$0 - 1 - 2 - 3$$

If yes, what did this look like?

4 ...demonstrated a higher level of engagement than usual?

$$0 - 1 - 2 - 3$$

If yes, please give examples

5 …gained increased confidence in the sessions and beyond the project?

$$0 - 1 - 2 - 3$$

If yes, please indicate how

6 …gained new skills?

$$0 - 1 - 2 - 3$$

If yes, what were these and how have they been demonstrated? If not, why do you think they haven't?

7 How important is the final outcome of this project to the young people?

$$0 - 1 - 2 - 3$$

How has this affected them?

Were there any unexpected outcomes?

What, using the information above, would you say is the distance travelled from the beginning of this project until now?

What wouldn't the children have had access to or opportunity of, if they had not done this project?

Appendix 5
Discussing Well-being and Learning – Prompt Questions from McLellan et al. (2012)

Adapted from McLellan et al. (2012) – Appendix 2.4 Pupil Interview Schedule (pp. 214–215) with permission from CCE.

Pupil interview schedule

This is based on the questions that researchers asked pupils as part of their study into the impact of Creative Partnerships on well-being. It is presented here as a possible exercise for teachers and pupils to consider together how the pupils feel about learning, both in and out of school, and how much autonomy, choice and decision making they think they have in their learning, all found to be important factors by McLellan et al. (2012) as discussed in Chapter 4.

Learning in different types of lessons

Recap past lessons and activities that the pupils took part in. Ask the pupils to describe:

- how typical these were;
- what happened in each;
- how they compare with each other.

Feelings inside school and outside school and what influences this

Do the pupils enjoy school? What about lessons? What particular things? What don't they enjoy in school?

How does school compare to life outside school?
Should life inside school be more like life outside or not?

Autonomy/Choice/Decision making

Explore the opportunities for the above in:

- different subjects;
- with different teachers/adults;
- in different outside lesson activities.

What about working with people other than teachers (e.g. practitioners)?

Talk/Dialogue

Explore the potential for group work and learning with others:

- in lessons;
- in other school activities.

Which subjects promote group work, which don't?
Do they work collaboratively outside of lessons? How does this work out?

How does discussion/group work help them learn or not learn? (in lessons and outside)

Relationship with teachers/other adults

Describe a teacher you have enjoyed learning things with (no names!), including what they teach or what their expertise is – what is it like being in their lessons?

Is there a teacher you have not enjoyed learning things with so much? What was it about their way of doing things that made it difficult for you to enjoy the process?

Describe learning with someone other than a teacher (inside or outside of school). How are they different from a teacher?

Should and could they be more similar?

Participation in school

What sort of things are you involved in school but outside of lessons? What have you organised yourselves?

What about outside of school? Do you get involved in anything outside of school?

Rounding off: How can school be improved? How could we improve opportunities for learning?

When the researchers asked these questions, they often used various visual prompts (e.g. photographs of lessons they had observed). This is something that teachers and pupils could work on creating, possibly as a preparation for conversations about different people's responses.

Appendix 6
Progression in Creativity – Field Trial 1 Notes to Teachers

Reproduced from Spencer et al. (2012) by permission of CCE.

These notes serve as a useful introduction to teachers interested in trying out the pupil-level assessment of creative dispositions which are discussed in detail in Chapter 8.

This project explores how we might monitor progress of creativity in pupils. For this short pilot study, we are asking you to:

- Focus on 6–12 pupils only in the years we specified.
- Attempt to map each child's profile at a single moment in time.
- Tell us what worked and what didn't in trying to do this.

We want to understand:

- How easily you are able to map a pupil onto our framework.
- How easily you are able to decide on, and gather, suitable decision-making evidence/data.
- What the sticking points are in the process we are asking you to try.
- How we could improve this process.

Our creativity framework breaks creativity down into five 'habits', each with three 'sub-habits'. Each of these sub-habits can become:

- Stronger (pupil requires less support and prompting to show sub-habit)
- Broader (pupil shows sub-habit in a range of activities and areas)
- Deeper (pupil's use of sub-habit becomes more skilful and complex)

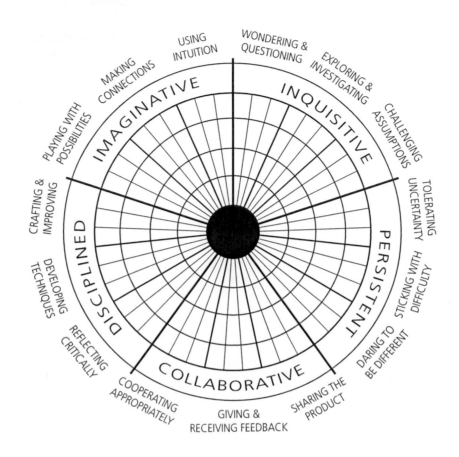

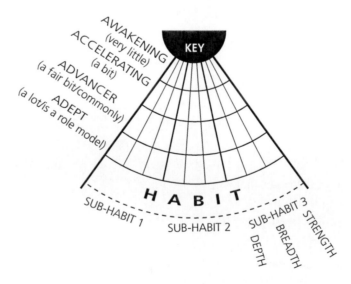

Progression in Creativity Tool, Version 1

For this short pilot we will look at one habit only (INQUISITIVE) with its three sub-habits:

- wondering and questioning
- exploring and investigating
- challenging assumptions

On a day of your choosing, please attempt to quantify 'strength', 'breadth', and 'depth' of each of the three aspects of pupils' inquisitiveness, at that time, on our two recording sheets. The whole framework is shown here:

- We are only going to look at the habit 'inquisitive'. Please look at the two recording sheets below, which we will ask you to compare.
- For the first pupil please identify (**on both of the two recording sheets**) how strong, broad, and deep you believe the pupil's current ability is in each of the three sub-habits.
- Please complete **at least one** of the recording sheets for each of your other selected pupils.
- Each sheet gives an example of how you might complete it.

Recording sheet 1

PUPIL NAME:

TEACHER NAME:

DATE:

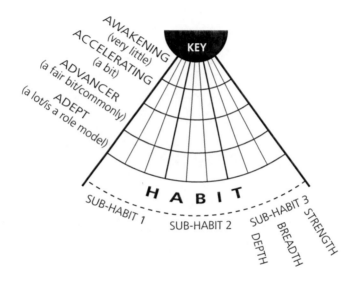

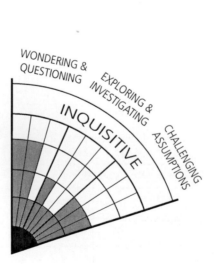

Recording sheet 2

CHILD NAME:

TEACHER NAME:

DATE:

**Forms of evidence
(teacher-led for pilot)**

Portfolios/passports
Diaries/journals/blogs
Learning stories/journeys
Teacher observations
Testimony from others
Evidence from 'products'
Reports
Reflective interviews
Progress reviews
Other

INQUISITIVE						
	STRENGTH (To what extent does pupil show this habit unsupported and unprompted?)		BREADTH (To what extent does pupil show this habit across a wide range of activities and areas?)		DEPTH (To what extent is pupil's use of this habit skilful and complex?)	
QUESTIONING (WONDER)						
INVESTIGATING (EXPLORE)						
CHALLENGING (DOUBT)						
(Example)	B	(detail evidence used)	A		A	

To quantify strength, breadth, and depth:

KEY				
	Very little; (Awakening)	A bit (Accelerating)	A fair bit; commonly (Advancing)	A lot; a role model (Adept)
Labels that work for you:				
(Example)	A	B	C	D

Notes

1   Figures for 2002 – 2008 from Creative Partnerships Monitoring Database report generated in January 2009. Figures for 2008 – 2011 from Creative Partnerships Projects Database report generated in March 2012. Both databases are owned by CCE.

2   Based on DfE website figure for Total number of schools in England = 24,507, as of January 2012.

Index